謹呈

積小為大

北尾吉孝

The SBI Group Vision and Strategy

The SBI Group Vision and Strategy

Continuously Evolving Management

Yoshitaka Kitao

BICENTENNIAL
1807
WILEY
2007
BICENTENNIAL

John Wiley & Sons, Inc.

Published by John Wiley & Sons, Inc., Hoboken, New Jersey.
Published simultaneously in Canada.

Wiley Bicentennial Logo: Richard J. Pacifico.

Library of Congress Cataloging-in-Publication Data:
Kitao, Yoshitaka.
    The SBI Group vision and strategy : continuously evolving management / Yoshitaka
Kitao.
        p.   cm.
    "Originally published in 2005 by Toyo Keizai Inc."—T.p. verso.
    ISBN 978-0-470-11798-9 (cloth)
    1. SBI Group—History.   2. Financial institutions—Japan—History—20th century.   3.
Financial institutions—Management.   4. Information technology—Economic
aspects—Japan.   I. Title.
HG187.J3K6   2007
332.10952—dc22
                                                                    2006037556

Printed in the United States of America.

10 9 8 7 6 5 4 3 2 1

CONTENTS

PREFACE

This book was written as a summary of my thoughts and actions over the past six years, since my pioneer days, so to speak, during which time I founded a company and nurtured it into a group of various companies. In this sense, one may consider this book a history of that company.

However, I note a few things that are different from a typical company history. First of all, not only am I the author of the book, but also the founder of the company and head of the group in its present form. Second, I have described the events mentioned from the view of one who was very much involved in them. Last, based on the preceding two points, this book is not just about consequences as historical facts; rather, it reveals my fundamental ideas and ways of thinking as the senior executive who helped in bringing about these consequences, as well as the process through which they have been realized.

I wrote this book with the intention that its readers would be primarily the officers and employees of our group companies. I hoped that reading this book would help them further strengthen their common bond. Yet I decided to have this book published because I thought that it might be helpful to others who are already in management positions in a variety of companies, who aspire to become executives, or who are contemplating becoming entrepreneurs. There are several reasons for this decision, which I discuss next.

First, this book covers most of the contemporary challenges that exist in corporate management. I believe that I discuss a wide range of topics, including corporate value; corporate organization; group management;

growth strategies, such as corporate acquisitions, joint ventures (JVs), and strategic alliances; strategies relating to competitiveness; and corporate social responsibility (CSR). Second, I have incorporated an analysis from various angles on management theory in the age of the Internet. Third, even though focused primarily on the financial industry, this book should serve as a useful reference, from a corporate management point of view, to persons who work in a wide range of industries. Last, I think I have, in my own way, digested to some degree and put into practice the academic achievements that I have gleaned from various books and scholarly articles through the expenditure of much time and energy.

This book is, in principle, a practical guide written by a senior executive who continues to take on various challenges today. The book is fundamentally different from books by economists and business critics, who compare companies to identify their common characteristics, or discuss and systematize common factors that have made companies successful. Having said this, I have no doubt that, without contact with the work of numerous scholars and business leaders, I would not have come to the ideas and strategies I have today. I am therefore profoundly grateful to all of my predecessors who have generously shared their management wisdom, knowledge, and lessons learned.

Yoshitaka Kitao

March 2007

The SBI Group Vision and Strategy

The Six Formative Years of the SBI Group

THE DAYS LEADING UP TO THE BIRTH OF THE SBI GROUP

The SBI Group traces its beginning as a group of companies that was formed around Softbank Finance Corporation, a wholly owned subsidiary of SOFTBANK CORP. and an integrated business management company. One can argue that Softbank Finance played a central role and was the leading figure in the finance-related operations within the SOFTBANK Group, which has professed to be at the forefront of the digital information revolution and has rolled out a wide variety of businesses, including the broadband business.

In the book I published about five and a half years ago entitled *E-fainansu no Chosen* (*Challenges of E-Finance*, Toyo Keizai Inc., Tokyo, 1999) and in its follow-up entitled *E-fainansu no Chosen II* (*Challenges of E-Finance II*, Toyo Keizai Inc., Tokyo, 2000), which came out about six months after the first book, I outlined in detail my thoughts regarding the businesses of the Softbank Finance Group when it came into being and my ideas about how I would build these businesses. I even introduced in great detail a number of specific business models relating to the innovative businesses of the group.

In the remainder of this section, I turn back the clock to the latter part of 1998, when I was envisioning the concept of creating a group.

At that time, I held the position of managing director and general manager of the Administration Group of SOFTBANK CORP., and my job was to oversee the Accounting Division, the Finance Division, the Legal and Credit Department, the IR Department, the Business Strategy Department, and other units of the company. With a total of only 55 employees in the Administration Group, I was at the helm of a group that was functioning in a manner similar to what is referred to as the cost center of a typical corporation (even though in reality the group generated about three billion yen in profit on a semiannual basis from foreign exchange dealing and other sources), while at the same time handling a series of large-scale acquisitions, investments, business partnerships, and so on as the chief strategic officer for Masayoshi Son, as well as the CFO of SOFTBANK CORP.

In September 1998, a resolution was passed at a meeting of the board of directors of SOFTBANK CORP. for the introduction of the holding company system, and the company subsequently became a pure holding company. At the same time, it announced that it would spin off each of its operating divisions as a subsidiary. In the business world today, there are a number of corporations making a move toward adopting the holding company system during the process of an industry-wide reorganization or consolidation. Such a move is nothing new in particular. However, in the business world in Japan at that time, I am fairly certain that SOFTBANK CORP. was making quite a pioneering decision in introducing the holding company system.

Softbank Finance Emerges to Connect the Internet to Financial Business

Against the backdrop of the transformation of SOFTBANK CORP. into a pure holding company, in April 1999, I took the entire 55 members of the Administration Group with me and formed a company named the Softbank Finance Corporation (see Exhibit I.1).

Through managing the businesses of SOFTBANK CORP., which

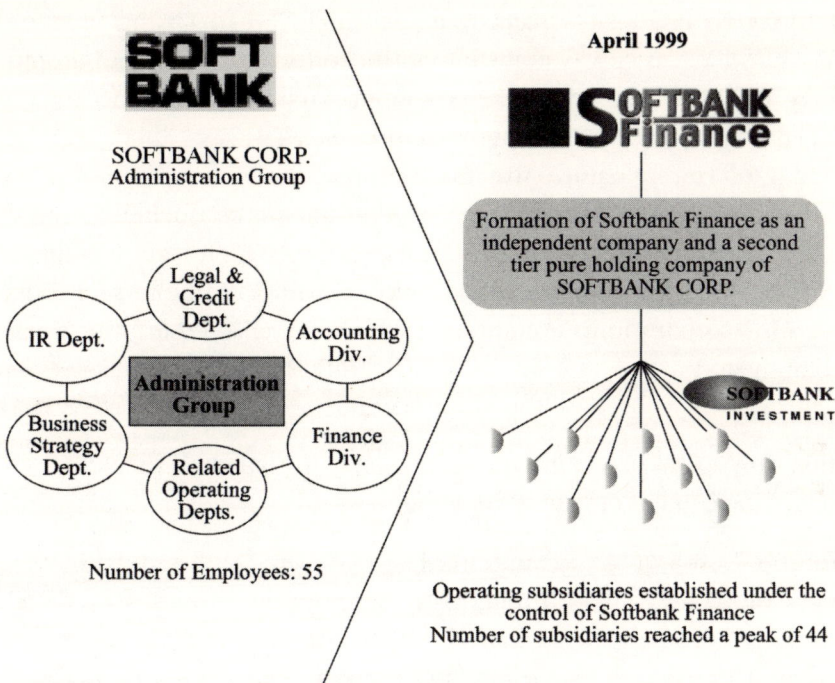

SOFT BANK

SOFTBANK CORP.
Administration Group

Legal & Credit Dept.

IR Dept.

Accounting Div.

Administration Group

Business Strategy Dept.

Finance Div.

Related Operating Depts.

Number of Employees: 55

April 1999

SOFTBANK Finance

Formation of Softbank Finance as an independent company and a second tier pure holding company of SOFTBANK CORP.

SOFTBANK INVESTMENT

Operating subsidiaries established under the control of Softbank Finance
Number of subsidiaries reached a peak of 44

EXHIBIT I.1   Formation of Softbank Finance (SBF)

was the leader in Internet businesses in Japan, as well as my experience of having come into contact with a number of U.S.-based Internet companies that were the leading players in this field in those days, I had an instinctual feeling about the enormous and inherent destructive power of the Internet. In addition, this power had a remarkable affinity with financial businesses, and I was certain that through the integration of the Internet into the field of finance we would be able to offer new financial products and services that could radically shake up the distorted order and system that had existed for years in the Japanese financial industry.

That is when I came up with the idea that by focusing on financial business as the main operating domain of Softbank Finance, I could drive a huge wedge into the financial industry using the Internet as a tool. Through the destructive power of the Internet, I wanted to correct the distorted financial system that existed in Japan so that it could transform itself into a system that would offer higher economic efficiency and improved convenience to investors and users of various financial services. I wanted to make a difference.

In addition, by nature, the financial market is so large that it is beyond comparison to the markets for other industries, such as computers, automobiles, and pharmaceutical products. Therefore, I believed that hidden in the financial market would be never-before-seen business opportunities for our company, which we believed to be a "financial innovator."

Within Only a Few Years After the Formation of the Softbank Finance Group, Nine Group Companies Go Public

After the founding of the Softbank Finance Corporation in April 1999, I went on to establish a number of operating subsidiaries in such a wide range of financial business fields that it would be fair to say that I covered every field in the industry with the exception of banking. I then took steps to make all of these subsidiaries part of our group (see Exhibit I.2).

The number of these group companies reached a peak of 44. As of the end of March 2006, there were 37 consolidated subsidiaries and 8 affiliated companies, which are accounted for under the equity method. Each of these companies has grown successful in its own business field.

The reason that the number of our consolidated subsidiaries stands at present at 37 is primarily due to the fact that we have engaged in a series of transactions in which we merged or consolidated certain subsidiaries. To this point, E-Bond Securities Co., Ltd. was the only subsidiary for which we made a management decision to liquidate.

There were also four companies that we sold to strategic partners. As a whole, however, what has become of the group today is that a great majority of the companies that we have established to date not only continue to stay in business with much success, but they are also expanding their businesses.

SBI Holdings

SBI Holdings, Inc.
<1st Section, Tokyo Stock Exchange: 8473>
URL: http://www.sbigroup.co.jp/
Description of business: Control and management of
the SBI Group through the ownership of shares, etc.

Asset Management Business:

SBI Investment Co., Ltd.

SBI Asset Management Co., Ltd.

SBI Capital Solutions Co., Ltd.

SBI CAPITAL Co., Ltd.

SBI Arsnova Research Co., Ltd.

SBI BROADBAND
CAPITAL K.K.

SBI Partners Co., Ltd.
<JASDAQ: 9653>
(Merger with SBI Holdings, Inc.
2006/03)

Brokerage and Investment Banking Business:

SBI E*TRADE SECURITIES
Co., Ltd.
<JASDAQ: 8701>

E*Trade Korea Co., Ltd.

SBI Securities Co., Ltd.
<Hercules: 8696>
(Wholly owned subsidiary of
SBI Holdings, Inc. 2006/3)

SBI Futures Co., Ltd.
<Hercules: 8735>

Financial Services Business:

Finance All Corporation
<Hercules: 8437>
(Merger with SBI Holdings, Inc.
2006/3)

SBI Lease Co., Ltd.

SBI Technology Co., Ltd.

Morningstar Japan K.K.
<Hercules: 4765>

SBI Equal Credit Co., Ltd.

SBI Business Solutions Co., Ltd.
(Formerly SBI Accounting Co., Ltd.)

SBI Benefit Systems Co., Ltd.

SBI VeriTrans Co., Ltd.
<Hercules: 3749>

SBI Financial Agency Co., Ltd.

SBI Promo Co., Ltd.

Gomez Consulting Co., Ltd.
< Hercules: 3813>

SBI artfolio Co., Ltd.

SBI Guarantee Co., Ltd.

SBI Mortgage Co., Ltd.

SBI Mortgage Consulting
Co., Ltd.
(Merger with SBI Mortgage
Co., Ltd. 2006/4)

Morningstar Asset
Management Co., Ltd.

E*Advisor Co., Ltd.
(Merger with Morningstar
Japan K.K.)

SBI Card Co., Ltd.

SBI Servicer Co., Ltd.

SBI Intechstra Co., Ltd.

(As of October 1, 2006)

EXHIBIT I.2   List of Principal SBI Group Companies

Furthermore, what deserves a special mention is that within only several years after the formation of the group there have already been nine group companies that have taken themselves public (see Exhibit I.3).

Even though this can be somewhat attributed to the fact that these companies were blessed with positive external factors, such as favorable market conditions for initial public offerings (IPOs), it is perhaps very rare in the business community in Japan to come across a corporate group that has accomplished initial public offerings made by nine of its group companies within such a short period of time. I take pride in the fact that such accomplishment itself may be considered an

· Group establishment date	April 1999
· Publicly-held group companies (at the maximum)	9 companies[1]
· Market capitalization of SBI Holdings, Inc.	816.4 billion yen[2]
· Market capitalization of publicly-held companies within the group[3]	1,819.3 billion yen[2]
· Market capitalization of the shareholdings of SBI in listed subsidiaries (equity interests)[4]	481.7 billion yen[2]
· Number of employees	Approx. 1,300 (consolidated basis)[2]
· SBI Group consolidated subsidiaries	37 companies[2]

(Unit: million yen)

	Operating Revenues	Recurring Profit	Net Income
Consolidated Results for Fiscal Year Ended March 2006	137,247	51,365	45,884

[1]: Shares of E*Trade Japan K.K. were listed in the past. Also included are five companies, which the group acquired or has a stake in. As of September 2006 two more companies, SBI Futures Co., Ltd., and Gomez Consulting Co., Ltd. were listed.
[2]: As of March 31, 2006.
[3]: Based on a simple summation, which includes SBI Holdings, Inc.
[4]: SBI E*TRADE SECURITIES Co., Ltd., Morningstar Japan K.K., SBI VeriTrans Co., Ltd., and Zephyr Co., Ltd.

EXHIBIT I.3   The SBI Group at Present

epoch-making achievement. We are also busy preparing for a scheduled initial public offering by another one or two of our other group companies before the end of the current fiscal year. Even though our original plan was to have three to four of our group companies make initial public offerings, we have changed our strategy. I explain the reason for this in Chapter 3.

MANAGEMENT BASES OF THE SBI GROUP AT PRESENT

To describe the operating bases of the SBI Group at present, I list the following companies, which I consider to be our principal business bases. (See also Exhibit I.4.)

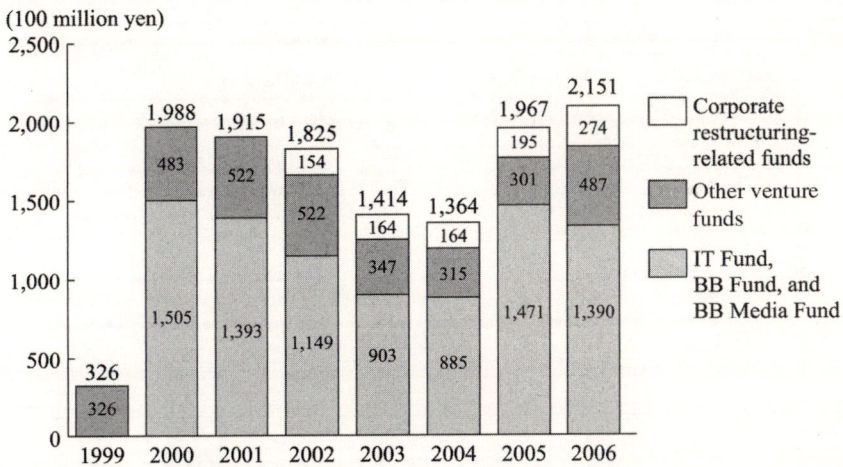

(100 million yen)

Legend:
- Corporate restructuring-related funds
- Other venture funds
- IT Fund, BB Fund, and BB Media Fund

Year	IT Fund, BB Fund, and BB Media Fund	Other venture funds	Corporate restructuring-related funds	Total
1999	326			326
2000	1,505	483		1,988
2001	1,393	522		1,915
2002	1,149	522	154	1,825
2003	903	347	164	1,414
2004	885	315	164	1,364
2005	1,471	301	195	1,967
2006	1,390	487	274	2,151

<Reference> Net assets of listed venture capital funds:

    JAFCO (Nomura affiliate): 179.7 billion yen

    NIF SMBC Ventures (Daiwa SMBC affiliate): 94.7 billion yen

    JAIC (Independent): 133.1 billion yen

    Sources: Data disclosed by each company as of March 31, 2006.

* The IT Fund represents the book value of its net assets, while the other funds are based on initial investment or initial commitment amounts.

EXHIBIT I.4   Changes in the Aggregate Operating Funds of the SBI Group

SBI Investment Co., Ltd.

Approximately 190 companies, primarily domestic and overseas institutional investors and operating entities, invest in venture capital funds managed by SBI Investment, which is a venture capital firm. As of March 2006, the aggregate book value amount of the net assets for these funds amounted to nearly 215.1 billion yen (see Exhibit I.4). The funds are invested, as of the end of March 2006, in a total of 258 companies, most of which are information technology (IT)-related companies. The performance of two funds, which have already been redeemed, was such that the internal rate of return (IRR) for both funds exceeded 20 percent (see Exhibit I.5).

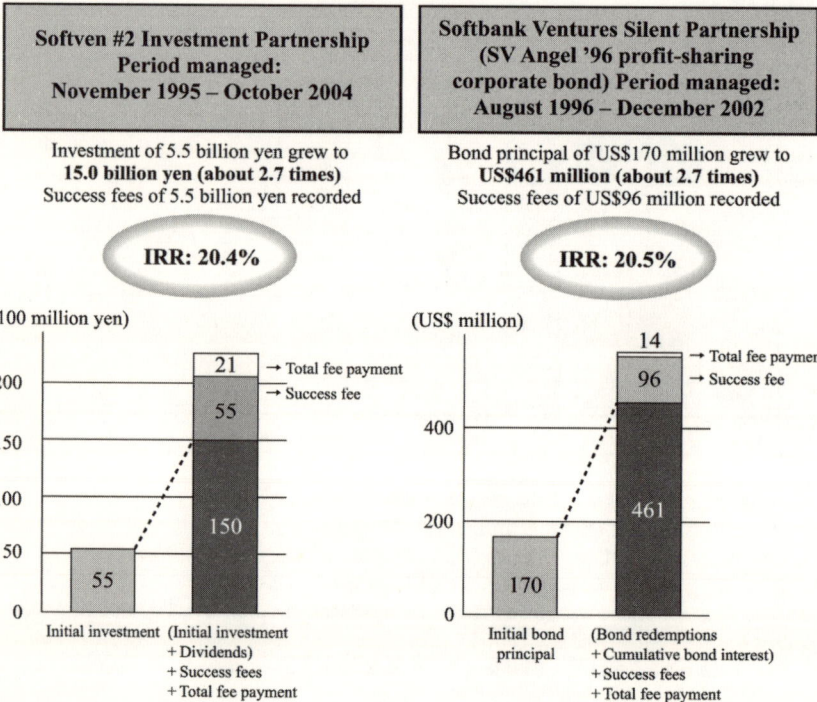

Softven #2 Investment Partnership Period managed: November 1995 – October 2004	**Softbank Ventures Silent Partnership (SV Angel '96 profit-sharing corporate bond) Period managed: August 1996 – December 2002**

Investment of 5.5 billion yen grew to
15.0 billion yen (about 2.7 times)
Success fees of 5.5 billion yen recorded

Bond principal of US$170 million grew to
US$461 million (about 2.7 times)
Success fees of US$96 million recorded

IRR: 20.4%   IRR: 20.5%

(100 million yen)

```
          21  → Total fee payment
200           → Success fee
          55

150

100       150

 50
     55

  0
  Initial investment   (Initial investment
                        + Dividends)
                        + Success fees
                        + Total fee payment
```

(US$ million)

```
              14  → Total fee payment
              96  → Success fee

400

              461
200
     170

  0
  Initial bond   (Bond redemptions
  principal      + Cumulative bond interest)
                 + Success fees
                 + Total fee payment
```

EXHIBIT I.5   Historical Performances of Redeemed Funds

SBI E*TRADE SECURITIES Co., Ltd.

SBI E*TRADE SECURITIES Co., Ltd., the leading pure-play Internet securities firm in Japan, as of March 31, 2006, maintains nearly 1,167,000 accounts (see Exhibit I.6) and approximately 4,582 billion yen in total deposits in customer accounts (see Exhibit I.7).

SBI Securities Co., Ltd.

Through acquisitions, SBI Securities Co., Ltd. (formerly World Nichiei Frontier Securities Co., Ltd.), a brick-and-mortar securities firm, and E*Trade Korea Co., Ltd., a pure-play Internet securities firm in South Korea, joined the SBI Group. As of March 31, 2006, SBI E*TRADE SECURITIES and SBI Securities together maintained 1,231,273 accounts and 5,110 billion yen in deposits in customer accounts.

Based on these figures, these two companies combined are ranked fourth in terms of the total number of securities accounts, following Nomura Securities, the Daiwa Securities Group, and the Nikko

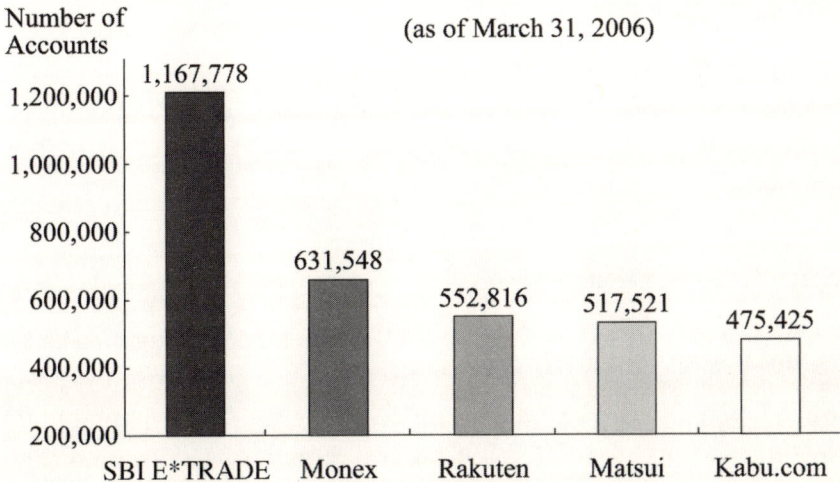

EXHIBIT I.6 Comparison of Online Securities Firms Based on the Number of Accounts

(100 million yen)

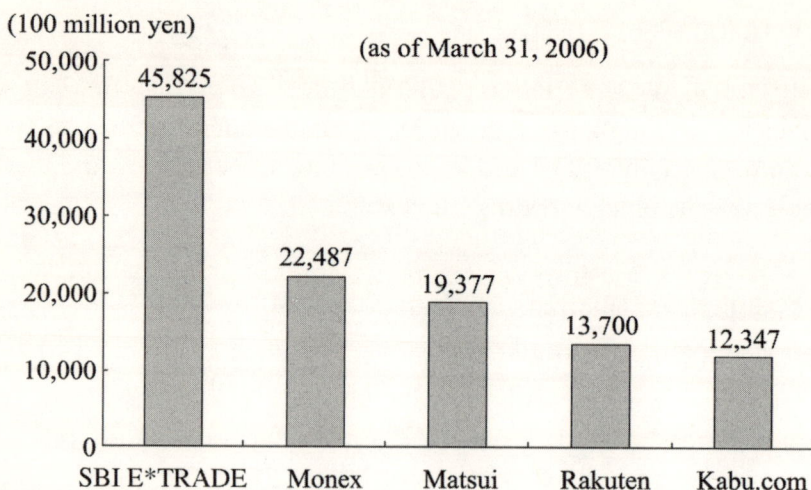

EXHIBIT I.7   Comparison of Online Securities Firms Based on Deposits in Customer Accounts

Securities Group. They are ranked at about seventh in terms of deposits in customer accounts.

Morningstar Japan K.K.

A company listed on the Hercules Market of the Osaka Securities Exchange, Morningstar Japan is engaged primarily in the rating of investment trusts in Japan. The company boasts close to 58,000 subscribers in its portfolio.

Finance All Corporation

A company that is also listed on the Hercules Market of the Osaka Securities Exchange, Finance All operates InsWeb, a comparison web site for insurance quotes, with 34 insurance companies participating in the providing of quotes (see Exhibit I.8 and Exhibit I.9), with more than 440,000 registered users.

The company was merged into SBI Holdings in March 2006.

The company also manages E-LOAN, a loan comparison web site, in partnership with as many as 72 financial institutions (see Exhibit I.10).

SBI Mortgage Co., Ltd.

In December 2004, SBI Mortgage Co., Ltd (formerly Good Mortgage Corporation), a housing loan company, began offering the "Flat 35," a housing loan provided in cooperation with the Government Housing Loan Corporation's efforts to promote housing loan securitization. Since then, as of the end of August 2006, the number of Flat 35 loans

- American International Underwriters (AIU) Insurance Co.
- Aioi Insurance Co., Ltd.
- American Home Assurance Company
- ACE Insurance
- SECOM General Insurance Co., Ltd.
- Assicurazioni Generalli S.p.A
- Sony Assurance Inc.
- Zurich Insurance Company
- Nissay Dowa General Insurance Co., Ltd.
- The Kyoei Fire & Marine Insurance Company, Limited
- Tokio Marine & Nichido Fire Insurance Co., Ltd.
- NIPPONKOA Insurance Co., Ltd.
- THE FUJI FIRE AND MARINE INSURANCE COMPANY, LIMITED
- AXA DIRECT Co., Ltd.
- Sonpo 24 Insurance Co., Ltd.
- SOMPO JAPAN INSURANCE INC.
- Mitsui Direct General Insurance Co., Ltd.
- Mitsui Sumitomo Insurance Company, Limited
- National Federation of Workers and Consumers Insurance Cooperatives (ZENROSAI)
- Nisshin Fire & Marine Insurance Co., Ltd.

Total: 20 companies (as of September 19, 2006)

EXHIBIT I.8 Insurance Companies Participating in the One-Stop Auto Insurance Quote Service

· American Family Life Assurance Company of Columbus (AFLAC)
· American Home Assurance Company
· American Life Insurance Company
· ORIX Life Insurance Corporation
· The Gibraltar Life Insurance Co., Ltd.
· SUMITOMO LIFE INSURANCE COMPANY
· Sompo Japan DIY Life Insurance Co., Ltd.
· Zurich Life Insurance Co., Ltd.
· Tokio Marine & Nichido Life Insurance Co., Ltd.
· TOMIN KYOSAI
· Nippon Life Insurance Company
· Manulife Life Insurance Company
· Mitsui Sumitomo Kirameki Life Insurance Company, Limited
· The Dai-ichi Mutual Life Insurance Company

Total: 14 companies (as of September 19, 2006)

EXHIBIT I.9   Insurance Companies Participating in the One-Stop Life Insurance Information Request Service

provided has grown rapidly, with a total loan balance exceeding 237.8 billion yen (see Exhibit I.11).

SBI Lease Co., Ltd.

SBI Lease is engaged in subleasing and syndication arrangement. The total lease balance of the company has grown to more than 34.8 billion yen as of the end of March 2006.

SBI Partners Co., Ltd.

A listed company on the JASDAQ, SBI Partners is engaged in a wide range of real estate-related businesses as an "innovator in the real estate industry," which takes on the creation and nurturing of new business

Partner Financial Institutions of E-LOAN

Aozora Bank, Ltd.	ACOM CO., LTD.
OME SHINKIN BANK	At-Loan Co., Ltd.
Ogaki Kyoritsu Bank, Ltd.	Ikko Co., Ltd.
Bank of Okinawa, Ltd.	INTER CO., LTD.
ORIX Trust and Banking Corporation	A.C.S. Finance Co., LTD
Kansai Urban Banking Corporation	GMO NETCARD, Inc.
GIFU BANK, Ltd.	SBI Equal Credit Co., Ltd.
GIFU SHINKIN BANK	SBI Mortgage
Kiyo Bank, Ltd.	OMC Card, Inc.
SHIZUOKA CHUO BANK	OX CAPITAL Co., Ltd.
JUROKU BANK, Ltd.	Station Finance Inc.
SHOKUSAN BANK	Sumisho Pocket Finance Corporation
Sumitomo Trust and Banking Co, Ltd.	SAISON FUNDEX CORPORATION
Senshu Bank, Ltd.	JCB Co., Ltd.
Sony Bank Inc.	SOMPO JAPAN INSURANCE INC.
Chiba Bank, Ltd.	Osaka Securities Finance Company, Ltd.
CHIBA SHINKIN BANK	TAKEFUJI CORPORATION
Chuo Mitsui Trust and Banking Co, Ltd.	DC Cash One, Ltd.
CHUKYO BANK, Ltd.	NISSIN CO., LTD.
TOMATO BANK, Ltd.	Japan Securities Finance
Nanto Bank, Ltd.	MUTOW CREDIT CO., LTD.
Incubator Bank of Japan, Ltd.	Orient Corporation
Hokkaido Bank, Ltd.	ORIX Credit Corporation
Mizuho Bank, Ltd.	CASCO CO., Ltd.
THE SHONAI BANK, LTD.	QUOQLOAN INC.
Sumitomo Mitsui Banking Corporation	CREDIA CO., LTD.
The Bank of Tokyo-Mitsubishi UFJ, Ltd.	CREDIT SAISON CO., LTD.
Mitsubishi UFJ Trust and banking Corporation	GE Consumer Finance Co., Ltd.
Minato Bank, Ltd.	Shinki Co., Ltd.
Musashino Bank, Ltd.	BUSINEXT CORPORATION
YACHIYO BANK, Ltd.	Hitachi Capital Corporation
The Bank of Yokohama, Ltd.	First Credit Corporation
	PRIVA Co., Ltd.
	Promise Co., Ltd.
	Sanyo Shinpan Finance Co., Ltd.
	Mitsui Sumitomo Insurance Company, Limited
	Mobit Co., Ltd.
	Rakuten Credit, Inc.
	Rakuten KC Co., Ltd.
	Resona Card Co., Ltd.

Total: 72 companies (as of September 19, 2006)

EXHIBIT I.10   Financial Institutions Participating in the Loan Comparison Web Site

(100 million yen)

**Housing loans
execution balance
as of August 31, 2006:
237.8 billion yen**

March, 2006
200 billion yen breakthrough

December, 2005
150 billion yen breakthrough

August, 2005
100 billion yen breakthrough

Tie-up with the Housing Loan Corporation
and beginning handling super 【flat 35】
December, 2004

2,000

1,500

1,000

500

0

Sep. Dec. Mar. Jun. Sep. Dec. Mar. Jun. Sep. Dec. Mar. Jun. Sep. Dec. Mar. Jun. Sep. Dec. Mar. Jun. Aug.
2001   2002   2003   2004   2005   2006

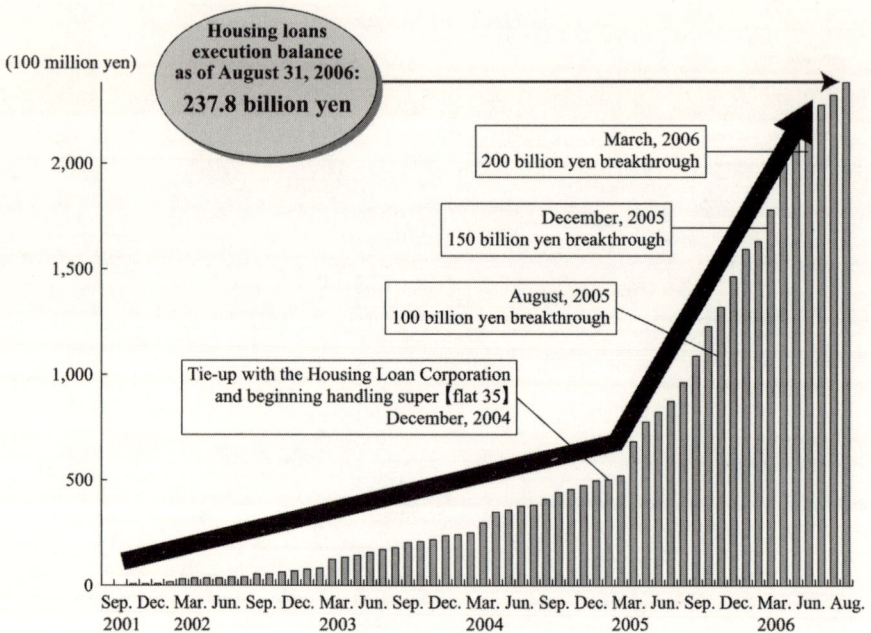

EXHIBIT I.11 Changes in Total Balance of Housing Loans Provided by SBI Mortgage

fields with the goal of realizing the "integration of real estate, finance, and IT." The company was merged into SBI Holdings in March 2006.

In the fiscal year ended June 2005, SBI Partners underwent a drastic change in shifting its focus from job placement-related businesses to real estate-related businesses. In less than a year since the launch of the new business format in November 2004, the size of the company's assets in the real estate investment business under its own account has grown to approximately 30.0 billion yen (including assets that are expected to be acquired), while the total amount of investment commitments in the real estate development business has reached more than 10.0 billion yen. In addition, the expected size of assets in the private placement real estate fund that is managed by the company has reached approximately 15.0 billion yen.

Suruga Bank Softbank Branch

The Suruga Bank Softbank Branch is a pioneer in the Internet banking business in Japan. Rather than establish a new pure-play Internet bank, the Suruga Bank Softbank Branch was established as a virtual entity to take advantage of the Internet banking business at a very early stage. The number of accounts held at the Suruga Bank Softbank Branch has already grown to more than 200,000.

From this overview, it is fairly apparent that the SBI Group has come to possess a variety of customer and operating bases within a wide range of fields.

CHAPTER 1

The Two Major Events That Brought About Structural Changes to the Financial Industry

When I was mapping out my ideas during the pioneer days of the SBI Group, the first thing I thought of was that if I was to create a new financial group and make a foray into the world of finance, I would have to gain a full insight into the near-future vision of the financial industry, and I would need to do so with as much precision as possible.

While taking on this task, I realized that there were two critical factors, both of which were to be unmistakably historic and large-scale, that would bring about structural changes to the financial industry. The first factor was, needless to say, the so-called Japanese Financial Big Bang, which refers to the sweeping financial reforms that were about to be finally realized in Japan some 20 years behind the United States. The other factor was the Internet Revolution, which would likely bring about the largest tidal shift since the Industrial Revolution, not only in the financial industry, but in virtually every aspect of human life.

These two changing events, both turning into huge waves at the same time, would transform the financial industry as we knew it into a completely different scene.

THE JAPANESE FINANCIAL BIG BANG

A Twenty-Year Delay in the Deregulation of Stock Brokerage Commissions

Let us now take a look at the so-called Japanese Financial Big Bang. The deregulation of commissions in stock brokerage, which was the symbolic element in financial reform, was implemented on May Day, May 1, 1975 in the United States, which was then followed by the United Kingdom on October 27, 1986. Japan, on the other hand, significantly lagged behind the United States by some 20 years in introducing a similar deregulation, which, however, was finally unveiled in November 1996 (see Exhibit 1.1). As a result of the complete liberalization of stock brokerage commissions in Japan, a number of Internet-based securities firms, such as E*Trade Securities (currently SBI E* TRADE SECURITIES), sprang up one after another. This new trend not only knocked brokerage commissions down below the traditional 1 percent level, but also dramatically repainted the scenery of the contemporary securities industry. Even today, the easing of regulations brought on by the Big Bang continues to sweep the industry. For example, in April 2004 the government introduced a new securities sales agency system.

Even though the new system did not apply to banks at that time, in December of the same year banks were allowed to engage in the securities sales agency business. Expressed in simpler terms, under this system, a party that is not a securities firm, upon executing a contract with a securities firm, would be allowed to solicit transactions as an intermediary in the selling and buying of securities, as well as the handling of the placement and offerings of securities.

To understand what the Japanese Financial Big Bang was aimed at, let us go back in time a little. It is generally believed that prior to the Big Bang, the basic framework for the financial system relating to banking and securities in Japan was established in the 1950s.

Indirect Financing Weighed Heavily in the Old Financial System

The national policy of Japan in the 1950s was to regain its footing after being beset by the ruins of the war as soon as possible, and once again

U.S.	U.K.	Japan
May 1975 **20 years before Japan** - **Abolition of the fixed-price commission system used by stock exchanges.** - Ensuring of inter-market competition as a mandatory condition. - Review of the policy to concentrate transactions on stock exchanges; establishment of a link between markets using the information technology possessed by each market; offering of sufficient trading information to investors; realization of ordering and execution in an optimal way. **1982** - Bank holding companies were given permission to acquire securities firms providing discount brokerage services. **1996** - Federal banks were given permission to allow subsidiaries to engage in the securities and insurance businesses. **November 1999** - Gramm-Leach-Bliley Act. A financial holding company system was introduced. - Complete removal of the barrier between banks and securities firms.	**October 1986** **10 years before Japan** - **Abolition of the fixed-price commission system used by stock exchanges.** - Abolition of the single-capacity system. - Dual capacity system became acceptable for both a market-making business and brokerage business to be operated by the same company. - Complete lifting of stock exchange membership restrictions. - Introduction of a new stock exchange system (SEAQ: Stock Exchange Automatic Quotation System) (abolition of trading floors). - Amendment of the Financial Services Act. **October 1997** - Establishment of the Financial Services Authority (FSA). **December 2001** - Implementation of the Financial Services and Market Act, which applies to all financial products. - Banks, securities firms and insurance companies are now regulated within the same framework.	**Financial reforms introduced in November 1996** - **Complete liberalization of stock brokerage commissions (effective October 1999).** - Shift from the licensing system to a registration system for securities firms (effective December 1998). - Banks were given permission to form securities firms as subsidiaries. - Abolition of trading floors at the Tokyo Stock Exchange (effective April 1999). **October 1997** Partial relaxation of the restrictions on the business scope of subsidiaries (banking and securities). **March 1998** - Complete lifting of the ban on the incorporation of financial holding companies (three industries; various business categories). **December 1998** - Shift to a registration system for the securities industry. Complete lifting of the ban on the sale of insurance by securities firms. Complete lifting of the ban on the over-the-counter sale of investment trusts by banks. **October 1999** Complete liberalization of the restrictions on the business scope of subsidiaries (all business categories). - Issuance and distribution of physical stocks by securities firms which are subsidiaries of banks. - Management of pension trusts by trust companies which are subsidiaries of securities firms. - Completion of the implementation of a system for establishing subsidiaries of insurance companies, banks, and securities companies (all business categories). **September 2003** Amendment of the Cabinet Office regulations relating to the operation of a bank and a securities company on the same retail premises. **April 2004** Security sales agency system becomes operational. **December 2004** Complete lifting of the ban on the operation of the securities sales agency business by banks.

EXHIBIT 1.1 Large-Scale Financial Reforms Introduced Since the First Financial Big Bang

catch up with as well as get ahead of the major industrial powers in the West. To achieve this goal, Japan needed to adopt a "priority production system" and focus primarily on developing its heavy and chemical industrial sectors. As a result, the government came up with a mechanism for enabling the efficient flow of funds that would be necessary for such development. A financial system that weighed heavily in "indirect financing" that was provided primarily by the banking system played a key role in the establishment of the said mechanism.

In 1952, the Long-Term Credit Bank Law was enacted, which became the basis for Japan's policy relating to the separation of long-term financing and short-term financing. The law allowed Japan's long-term credit banks, such as the Industrial Bank of Japan, to take in long-term funds through the issuance of financial debentures, while major city banks and regional banks took in short-term deposits and then lent short-term funds to enterprises. In other words, long-term financing was undertaken separately from short-term financing.

The Securities and Exchange Law that was enacted in 1948, on the other hand, set forth the separation of operations between banks and securities firms. Through this law, and under the direction and guidance of the government, a financial system weighted heavily in indirect financing started to materialize.

In addition, in 1951 the Shinkin Bank Law and the Mutual Savings (Sougo) Bank Law were implemented, both of which helped to clarify the position of medium- and small-sized business financial institutions that played a major role in supplying funds to medium- and small-sized enterprises. Furthermore, in the early 1950s the government created a series of public financial institutions, such as the Government Housing Loan Corporation (1950), Agriculture, Forestry and Fisheries Finance Corporation (1953), and Japan Finance Corporation for Small and Medium Enterprise (1953). The creation of these institutions at such a rapid pace stemmed from the fact that the main goal of private-sector banks at that time was to fulfill the funding needs of large corporations, so it was necessary to provide the funds needed in those areas where these banks were not able to. The funds that flowed into public financial institutions came from the deposits that had been collected through the postal savings system and then deposited with the Ministry of Finance.

The basic framework for insurance is actually much older than its counterpart in the banking and securities industries, and it was originally based on the former Insurance Business Law, which was enacted in 1939. This law was created using German insurance law as its guideline after Japan had experienced a crisis in its financial sector during which a number of insurance companies collapsed in succession. Until the law was amended, which came finally after a half century, the life insurance sector had remained completely separated from other financial industries in an environment where competition was highly restricted by the Japanese Ministry of Finance.

The Disappearance of the Barriers between Financial Institutions

Now that I have touched upon the situation that prevailed in the past, I talk about what the Japanese Financial Big Bang is basically trying to achieve. In the past, under the Japanese legal system, financial institutions have been historically compartmentalized into various categories, such as commercial banks, long-term credit banks, trust banks, securities firms, and insurance companies. One goal of this financial reform is to gradually lower and eventually completely remove the barriers that exist among these various categories (see Exhibit 1.2). Even I, who have spent many years working at a securities firm, would never have imagined that banks would one day be selling stock, even over the counter. To be honest, I was in fact putting quite a lot of effort into preventing banks from doing just that.

I think that what we will be seeing next is the likelihood that banks will eventually start underwriting securities. When that happens, it will mean that the barriers will have truly come down.

In principle, we can explain any type of financial product based on the risk and return that is associated with it. From the perspective of the customer, it would save us a lot of running around if we were able to take care of everything at one location, rather than having to make separate trips to the banks, securities firms, insurance companies, and so on,

Commercial Banks

Long-Term Credit Banks

Collapse of the boundaries as a result of the easing of regulations

Creation of integrated financial companies that provide a variety of financial services

Trust and Banking Companies

Diversification of investment needs based on risk and return

Securities Firms

Insurance Companies

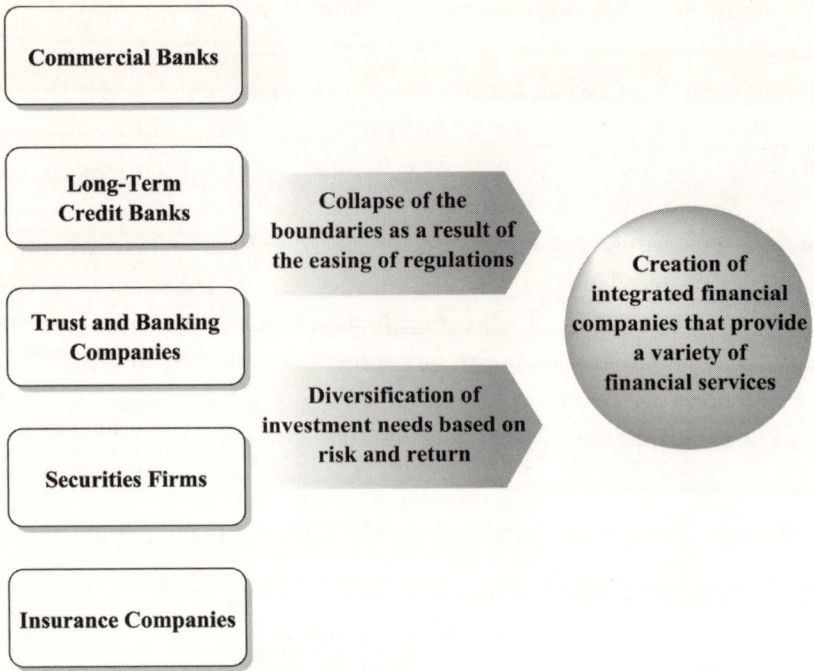

EXHIBIT 1.2   Collapse of the Boundaries in the Financial Industry Paves the Way for the Creation of Integrated Financial Companies

and deal with each of these individually. The best solution would be to create integrated financial companies that would be able to provide all the financial services and products. There is no doubt in my mind that we are headed toward the realization of such companies in the future.

Internet Revolution

In financial business, transactions do not require that goods be physically exchanged. Rather, transactions simply involve the exchange of figures or data. In this sense, the industry can even be thought of as akin to the information industry, involving very information-intensive businesses. It is no exaggeration to say that there are no other industries that have as much of an affinity with the Internet as the financial industry has.

Direct Targeting of Financial Institutions Through the Internet

Five Characteristics of the Internet. The Internet has the five following distinguishing characteristics: low cost, real time, multimedia, interactivity, and global reach. (See Exhibit 1.3.)

It is such characteristics as these that can have a head-on impact on the management of financial institutions. As an example of the Internet being low-cost, the current commissions that are earned by SBI E*TRADE SECURITIES have fallen below the 1 percent level, which was the going rate prior to the deregulation of brokerage commissions. This attests to the claim that the Internet truly does possess an incredible price-cutting power (see Exhibit 1.4).

What is more important is that despite such significant fall in commissions, SBI E*TRADE SECURITIES continues to generate a large

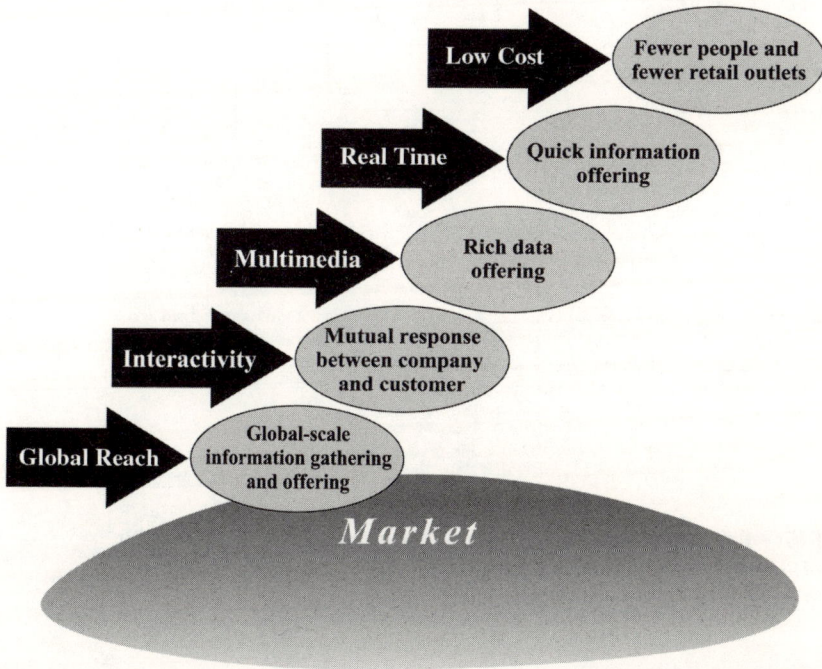

EXHIBIT 1.3   Five Market-Changing Characteristics of the Internet

Comparison of the Stock Brokerage Commissions
of Various Companies (Spot and Limit Orders)
* In the case of a spot contract value of 1 million yen with a price limit.

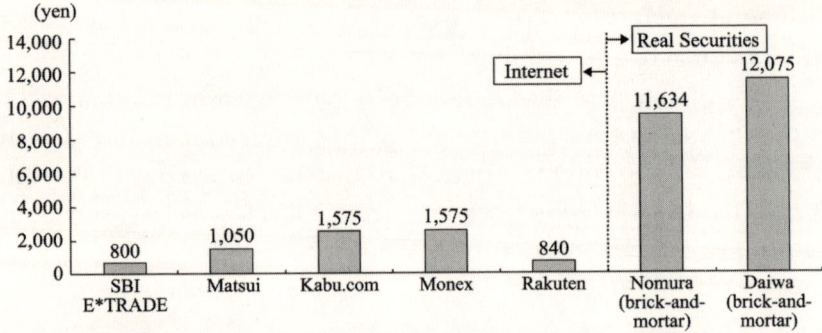

(yen)

	SBI E*TRADE	Matsui[*1]	Kabu.com	Monex	Rakuten	Nomura (brick-and-mortar)[*2]	Daiwa (brick-and-mortar)
1 million yen	800	1,050	1,575	1,575	840	11,634	12,075
3 million yen	1,500	3,150	2,415	4,725	1,575	28,434	30,555
5 million yen	1,500	5,250	2,415	7,875	1,575	44,604	49,035

Notes: The above figures represent commissions on the contracted amount per order in a spot
trade with a price limit.
Special promotional commissions are not included.
The figures are calculated based on the commission schedules that were released by all
of the above companies prior to September 20, 2006.

* 1: Commission charged on the total contract value per day (no commission charged per
trade).
* 2: Applicable to a retail customer who opens a custody account and enters into a
comprehensive securities services contract.

(as of September 20, 2006)

EXHIBIT 1.4   Price-Cutting in Brokerage Commissions Made Possible by
the Internet

recurring profit in excess of 30.0 billion yen per year (fiscal year ended March 31, 2006).

Trade-Off between "Richness" and "Reach." Let us now talk about how such large amounts of profit may be generated.

To understand in a systematic manner what the Internet Revolution has produced, it will perhaps be helpful to employ the concepts of "richness" and "reach." These concepts were clearly introduced by Phillip Evans and Thomas Wurster in the *Harvard Business Review* published in 1997. The "richness" of information refers to the quality of information, while "reach" refers to the number of persons who share that information.

It has been argued for many years that there was a trade-off (choice between only two things) between richness and reach. In the world of business administration, the term "marketing mix" often comes up in reference to the issue as to how management resources relating to information sharing purposes should be allocated given this trade-off. For example, consider the scenario wherein the seller of a product is trying to persuade consumers to spend money to buy it. In this scenario, the reach to consumers through a TV advertisement will be very extensive, while the richness in this case will be grossly static as the information conveyed through the advertisement will be extremely limited due to the very high hourly advertisement fee.

In the case of direct-mail advertising, on the other hand, while its reach may be far inferior to that of a TV advertisement, it is possible that, in terms of richness, the information delivered through this method will be much superior to TV advertising. In the case where a salesperson directly persuades a consumer to buy a product, the richness of the information delivered will be more convincing, while its reach extends to only a few persons at a time.

Information Asymmetry and the Trade-Off. It may be said that an "information asymmetry" was also generated from the richness/reach trade-off.

Let us consider an example by using a securities firm and the investors who are the clients of the firm. There are usually analysts at each securities firm. Analysts visit various companies and meet with the top management executives and officers responsible for accounting and finance in order to collect information. This suggests that there is a huge gap between a securities firm and its client investors in terms of the amount of information on the companies that are visited by the analysts of that firm.

Because it required an enormous amount of effort, time, and cost to obtain such information that contained a high level of richness, the reach to the audience of such information was naturally limited to analysts and professionals such as banks with which the companies had relationships. Such severe restriction on the reach to an audience was not very desirable from the point of view of investor relations (IR) activities of the companies distributing the information. Naturally, a company would want to extend its reach as far as possible and engage in extensive public relations activities for not only its existing shareholders, but also its potential investors so that it could be ensured that the company would be neither overvalued nor undervalued in the capital market.

However, without the means to deliver information extensively at a low cost, most companies had no choice but to give up on the idea of extending their reach of information to a larger audience. Such information asymmetry was, in many cases, generated from the trade-off between the richness and reach of information, and was, more likely than not, used as a source of profit for those who possessed more information than others (see Exhibit 1.5).

Collapse of the Trade-Off Brought On by Digital Information Goods

Along with the progress of the Internet Revolution, the trade-off relationship between richness and reach, which has been the foundation for the old economic principle of information, began to gradually dissolve. As a result, any information asymmetry also began to melt down. The reason why the trade-off relationship gradually dissolved has a lot to do with the characteristics of digital information goods. These characteristics are as follows.

Choice between information quantity and quality (trade-off)

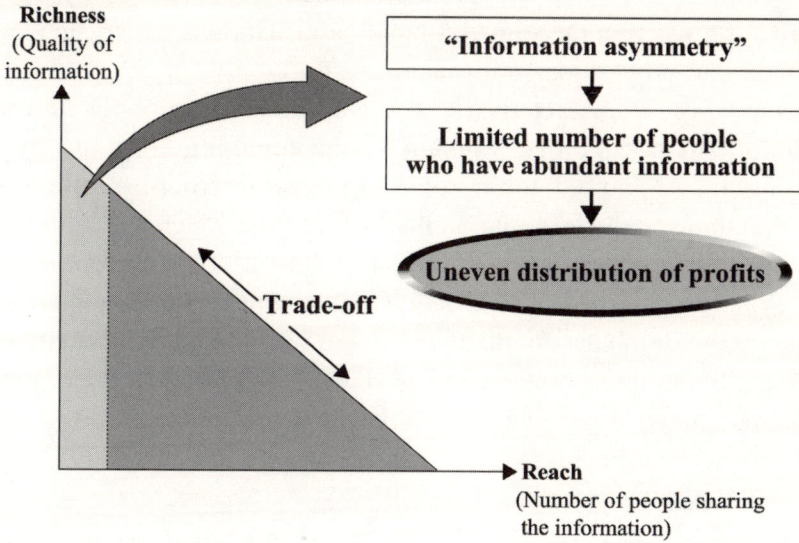

EXHIBIT 1.5   Economic Principle of Information (Prior to the Age of the Internet)

Richness Enhanced by the Characteristics of Digital Information Goods. First of all, digital information goods have exceedingly low variable costs when it comes to the distribution of information. This is largely due to the fact that the costs of reproduction, saving, and transmission for digital information have come down to a level whereby they can be pretty much ignored. Second, charges collected in the reproduction and distribution of digital information goods tend to level off at a certain price.

Because of these two characteristics, digital information goods are often provided free of charge despite the fact that they have a high cost of production and an economic value.

When digital information having such unique characteristics is transmitted through the Internet, it will immediately expand the previously existing market sphere, and the reach to the audience is dramatically broadened. At the same time, it is able to enhance the richness of the information. Furthermore, if "economies of network," which is another characteristic of digital information goods, comes into play, then the richness of the information will be further enhanced. The term "economies of network" refers to a phenomenon brought on by digital information wherein the value of digital information is enhanced when it is linked to other digital information.

Due to these characteristics of digital information goods and the evolution of the Internet community, the trade-off relationship between richness and reach has ceased to exist. Internet-based companies that transmit the information that balances both richness and reach and offer trading tools to their audiences (SBI E* TRADE SECURITIES being one of these firms) have been able to achieve a dramatic growth in their number of customers. By offering a wide range of products and releasing high-quality information with respect to these products, these companies have been able to respond to diversified customer needs and expand their businesses (see Exhibit 1.6).

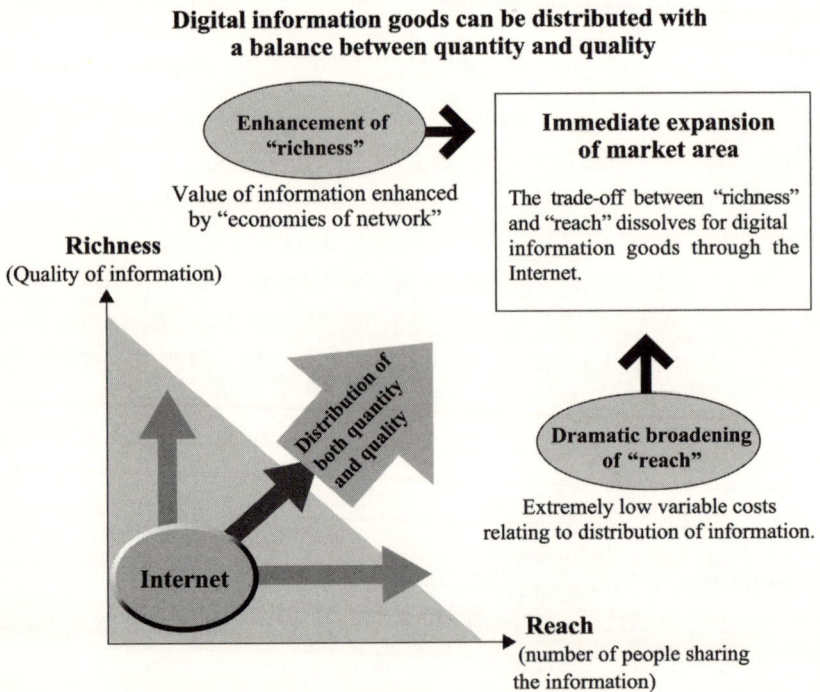

Digital information goods can be distributed with a balance between quantity and quality

Enhancement of "richness"

Value of information enhanced by "economies of network"

Richness
(Quality of information)

Immediate expansion of market area

The trade-off between "richness" and "reach" dissolves for digital information goods through the Internet.

Distribution of both quantity and quality

Internet

Dramatic broadening of "reach"

Extremely low variable costs relating to distribution of information.

Reach
(number of people sharing the information)

EXHIBIT 1.6   Economic Principle of Information (The Internet Age)

Having said that, I say it is fairly obvious that the evaporation of the trade-off relationship between richness and reach, and as a result, the collapse of information asymmetry have in fact had the overall effect of bringing far more benefits to consumers and investors who trade by using the information and trading tools that are provided by Internet-based companies in comparison to the benefits experienced by these Internet companies.

What is particularly interesting is that as the Internet Revolution and the Japanese Financial Big Bang were unfolding almost in parallel, the financial industry was experiencing a great upheaval out of which came a trend that greatly favors consumers and investors.

CUSTOMER-CENTRIC MARKETPLACE AND BUSINESS OPPORTUNITIES

The Internet Revolution has enabled consumers and investors to obtain adequate information without having to put forth much effort or spend much time and money, and to make purchases or investments based on that information. When consumers and investors continue to obtain adequate information, they become more and more knowledgeable and intelligent. This process will eventually give birth to a "customer-centric marketplace." As a consequence, consumer and investor sovereignty will be established (see Exhibit 1.7).

This said, consumers and investors do not always have everything worked out for them or are not always free from problems. They inevitably find themselves caught in a flood of information. This is the kind of situation that is best described by the saying, "Too much spoils, too little does not satisfy."

Caught in this flood of information and with very limited human cognitive ability, consumers will soon begin to seek out those who specialize in performing searches on or compiling the overflow of information. Through this process will arise new business opportunities.

In conclusion of this section, I cite several paragraphs from *The Theory of Economic Development* (translated from the German by Redvers Opie, Harvard University Press, Cambridge, Massachusetts, 1934) and *Capitalism, Socialism, and Democracy* by J.A. Schumpeter (Harper

Consumers and personal investors become the largest beneficiary

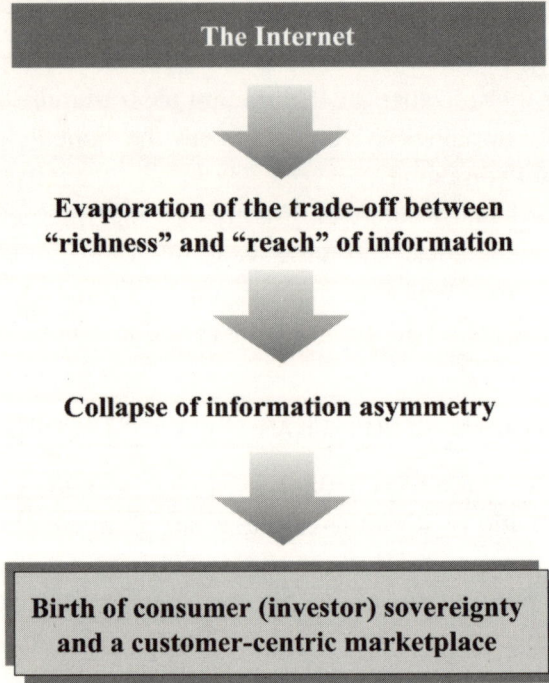

The Internet

↓

Evaporation of the trade-off between "richness" and "reach" of information

↓

Collapse of information asymmetry

↓

Birth of consumer (investor) sovereignty and a customer-centric marketplace

EXHIBIT 1.7   Birth of a Customer-Centric Marketplace

& Row, New York, 1942), one of the most prominent economists of the twentieth century:

> The fundamental impulse that sets and keeps the capitalist engine in motion comes from the new consumers' goods, the new methods of production or transportation, the new markets, the new forms of industrial organization that capitalist enterprise creates.
>
> The opening up of new markets, foreign or domestic, and the organizational development from the craft shop and factory to such concerns as U.S. Steel illustrate the same process of industrial mutation—if I may use that biological term—that incessantly revolutionizes the economic structure from within, incessantly destroying the old one, inces-

santly creating a new one. This process of Creative Destruction is the essential fact about capitalism. It is what capitalism consists in and what every capitalist concern has got to live in.

In capitalist reality . . . it is . . . competition from the new commodity, the new technology, the new source of supply, the new type of organization—competition which commands a decisive cost or quality advantage and which strikes not at the margins of the profits and the outputs of the existing firms but at their foundations and their very lives.

Situations emerge in the process of creative destruction in which many firms may have to perish that nevertheless would be able to live on vigorously and usefully if they could weather a particular storm.

It is that kind of change arising from within the system which so displaces its equilibrium point that the new one cannot be reached from the old one by infinitesimal steps. Add successively as many mail coaches as you please, you will never get a railway thereby.

As clearly suggested by these words of Schumpeter, it is likely that through the "new products, new technologies, new markets, new types of industry organization, and so on" created by the Internet, a process of "creative destruction" will be brought on by the Internet in every part of the world with a rapidity that we have never before witnessed.

The industry in which this process will take place first will likely be the financial industry, which is often said to have the highest affinity with the Internet of all industries.

Near-Future Vision of Financial Businesses: Integrated Financial Company

I stated earlier that the direction of the financial industry in the near future would be such that as a result of the Financial Big Bang traditional barriers among financial institutions will continue to be scrapped at a very fast speed.

In principle, as I also mentioned earlier, we can explain any type of financial product based on the risk and return that is associated with it. Therefore, from the customers' standpoint, rather than having to make separate trips to banks, securities firms, insurance companies, and so on, and dealing with each of these individually, a convenient one-stop location, where everything needed can be done reliably without the customer having to run around to different locations, is in much demand.

Triple Service Offering (see Exhibit 1.8)

One-Stop Service. It would be ideal to create integrated financial companies that provide all the financial services and products that we need, and this is most likely the direction in which future financial companies are headed. In other words, a one-stop service would be realized.

One-List Service. Another direction where the industry is headed is the one-list service.

For example, traditionally when we go to a bank to ask about a housing loan, the bank will normally speak only about its own products and not mention the products of other banks. However, the continuing advancement of the Internet has enabled us to compare the

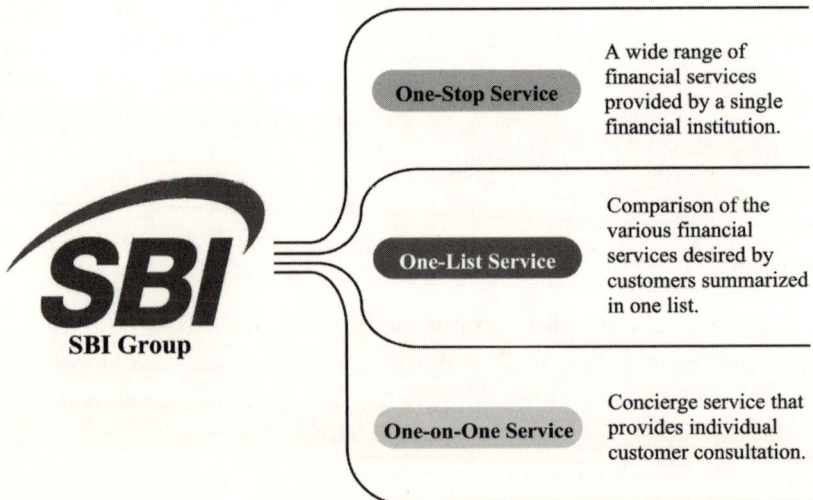

SBI

SBI Group

One-Stop Service — A wide range of financial services provided by a single financial institution.

One-List Service — Comparison of the various financial services desired by customers summarized in one list.

One-on-One Service — Concierge service that provides individual customer consultation.

EXHIBIT 1.8   Triple Service Offering

products of various banks and select one that is most appropriate for us in terms of interest rate and other conditions. There are now companies that offer web sites through which we can obtain such information on one list.

As this trend continues to unfold, we are now entering the age wherein customers may choose financial institutions based on the information that is obtained on their own from various comparison web sites and other sources on the Internet. Customers will no longer have to fulfill their banking needs with a bank simply because it happens to be near their home and they have maintained a business relationship with it over the years, since they are now able to check out the products, services, and costs of other banks all on their own. Therefore, it can be said that the future looks increasingly promising for the type of financial business that specializes in offering various financial information on one list through comparison sites.

One-on-One Service. In an Internet community that holds on to its customer-centric principle, it will most likely become more and more important to offer one-on-one service which will become more sophisticated than ever before. Financial institutions will have to assess the needs of each and every customer and offer the best financial services in accordance with these needs.

Creation of a Network Value

The Comprehensive Offering of Information, Goods, and Services. In the age of the Internet, companies will ultimately have to create a "network value" that will enable the comprehensive offering of information, goods, and services.

Although "network value" is a term that I coined myself, it was Toshifumi Suzuki, Chairman of Seven & i Holdings Co., Ltd. (formerly Ito Yokado), who once said, "We are no longer in the era of price appeal. We are now entering into an era of value appeal." What he meant was that times are changing and companies will no longer be able to sell products simply because they are priced low. In other words, in the era of value appeal, consumers will no longer pay for products that are not worth their money (see Exhibit 1.9).

The term "network value" reflects my belief that in the age of the Internet it is no longer good enough to offer a product in line with its value alone. For example, let us say that there is a fellow who wants to buy a house. The first thing he has to do is look up real estate information, or obtain housing loan information such as what a financial institution offers, the most reasonable interest rate, and so on.

He may also have to find out if the property that he is interested in is close to schools, hospitals, parks and so on, or what the local environment is like. It is apparent that he will have to obtain a variety of information. When he actually buys the house and it is time to move, he

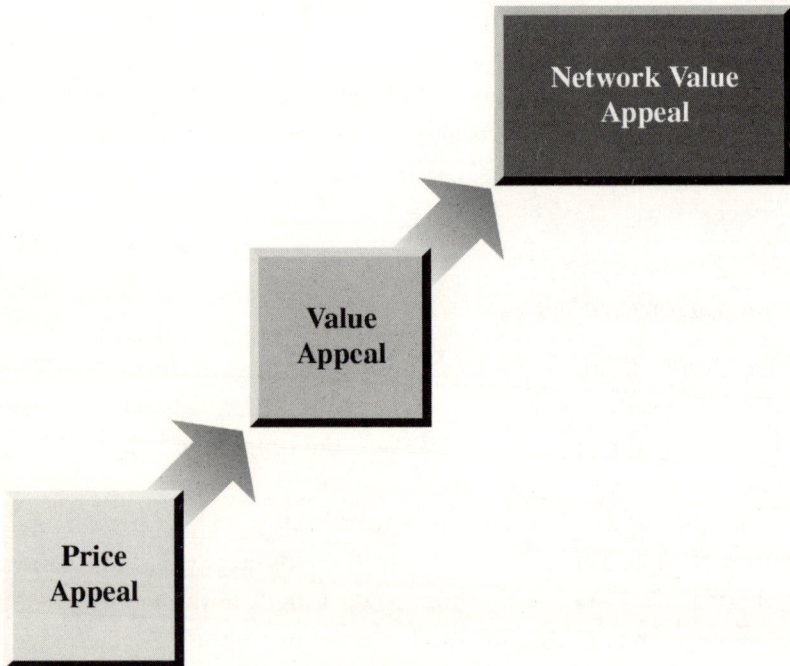

EXHIBIT 1.9   Flow of Network Value Appeal

will then need to possess information on relocation, interior designers, and so on (see Exhibit 1.10).

If our group were able to offer every piece of information needed while other financial institutions were not able to, then whom would these customers select? The answer to this question is quite obvious. I believe that a network value in the true sense of the word can be created by offering a network that provides information on the various values of goods and services and provides effective support for customers in their buying decisions (see Exhibit 1.11). We, of course, provide the kinds of goods and services at a very competitive or cheaper price to our customers through our own channels and affiliates. Only those financial institutions that can offer such a value will become the surviving winners.

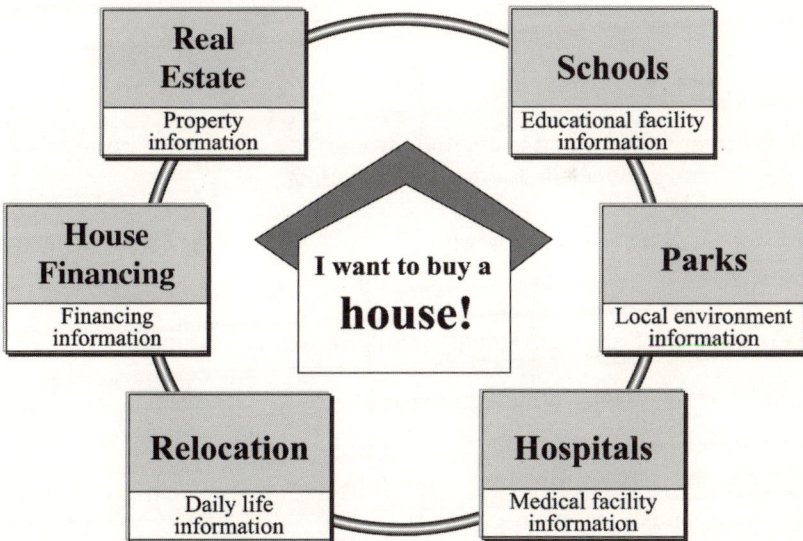

Real Estate	Schools
Property information	Educational facility information

I want to buy a **house!**

House Financing	Parks
Financing information	Local environment information

Relocation	Hospitals
Daily life information	Medical facility information

A network is built to offer a variety of information that is needed by those who wish to buy a house and to provide effective support for their buying decisions.

EXHIBIT 1.10   Example of the Creation of Network Value

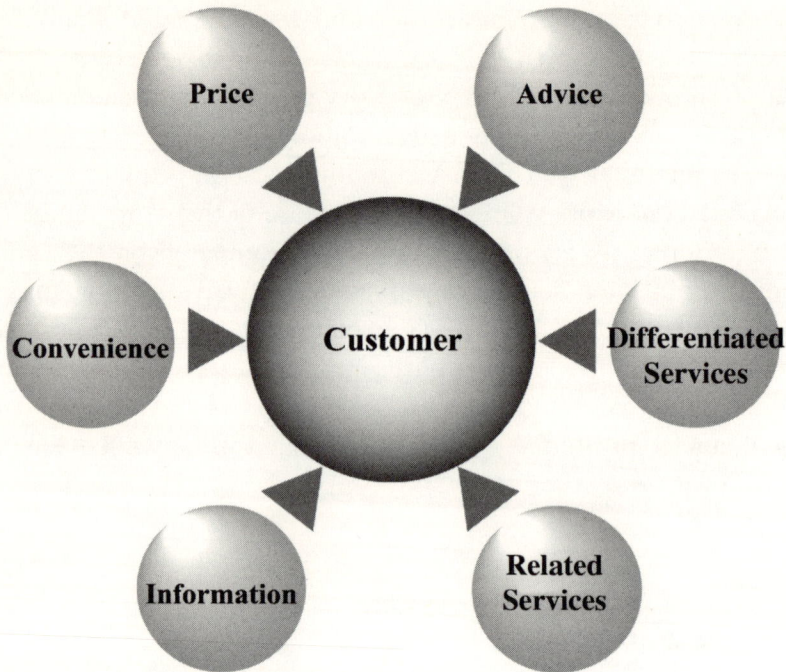

Customer value-added is created through the offering of information, goods, and services in an integrated manner.

EXHIBIT 1.11   Offering of the Network Value Demanded in the Age of the Internet

The Concept of "Corporate Value" of the SBI Group Companies

Perpetually Evolving Values of Group Companies. In my book entitled "*Kachi Sozo*" *no Keiei* ("*Value Creation*" *Management*, Toyo Keizai Inc., Tokyo, 1997), I discuss the subject of "corporate value" and explain that cash flow is the source of value creation. However, since the release of this book, I have read a number of business books and literature on corporate value and have managed a number of Internet-based companies. I have also come upon a slew of business results released by the Internet-based companies, in which funds managed by the SBI Group have been invested. I have now come to the conclusion that it is inappropriate to define corporate value in a textbook manner as I do in that book.

While thinking of how to redefine this term, I found the clue to this new definition in a book by R. S. Kaplan of Harvard University and D. P. Norton of Claremont Graduate University entitled *Balanced Scorecard* (translated by Takeo Yoshikawa, Japan Productivity Center for Socio-Economic Development, Tokyo, 1997).

The authors of the book propose a solution to the problem of how intangible "soft" assets, such as brands and other intellectual capital, are not taken into consideration on traditional financial statements. In other words, these assets are treated as having zero value. In addition to the conventional financial indicators, the Balanced Scorecard method incorporates indicators for management performance with respect to customers, internal business processes, and organizational learning and growth. The authors argue that the traditional financial indicators suggest only the outcomes of the past, and they propose an approach, through the use of the Balanced Scorecard method, to reflect types of corporate behavior that will generate cash flows in the future.

For example, with respect to customers, the Balanced Scorecard method allows a company to grasp the level of customer satisfaction by establishing specific indicators relating to product quality, services, and lead time, among other things.

With respect to internal business processes, the method incorporates indicators for clarifying what needs to be done to raise the level of satisfaction among customers and shareholders. For example, these indicators relate to the time required for production and the rate of defective goods.

For organizational learning and growth perspective, the method incorporates indicators for measuring the ability of a company to reform and improve itself in order to realize its vision. For example, the method uses an indicator relating to improvements in the ratio of sales of new products to total sales.

Skandia Insurance Company Ltd., the largest insurance company in northern Europe, employs an approach similar to the Balanced Scorecard method, which is based on a technique that was developed by Intellectual Capital Services Ltd. The approach used by Skandia classifies the market value of a company into "shareholders' equity" in the context of tax accounting, which is reported on the balance sheet, and "intellectual capital," which is not recognized on the financial statements. Furthermore, "intellectual capital" is comprised of four types of capital: human capital, customer capital, renewal and development capital, and process capital. This approach, like the approach used by Kaplan and Norton, is aimed at measuring the "soft" elements that do not appear on financial statements, and as a result, the true value of a company.

Corporate Value Is an Aggregation of Customer Value, Shareholder Value, and Human Capital (Officers and Employees) Value. In the past, of the aforementioned five components of capital, I paid attention only to shareholders' equity. However, I have come to realize that shareholders' equity by itself is insufficient, and that human capital and customer capital also need to be taken into consideration, because all three of these components of capital are indispensable for the continuing existence and development of a company. If it has all of these three capital components, then the remaining renewal and development capital and process capital can be generated from them. As a result, I now believe that corporate value is an aggregate of customer value, shareholder value, and human capital (officers and employees) value (see Exhibit 1.12).

Customer Value. Customer value is one that is offered by a company and represents the intrinsic value of the goods and services offered by that company. It may also be considered a cash flow from the customers who pay for the goods and services offered by the company. Customer value has a particularly significant value for those companies that must strictly adhere to a customer-centric principle in order to survive in the age of the Internet. It may even be said that the customer-centric principle has brought on drastic changes in business structures and has had a significant impact on the concept of value, which forms the basis of any management strategy.

However, when you think about it, customers are the source of cash flow that is received by a company, and value is created because customers pay for the goods offered by that company. Therefore, the

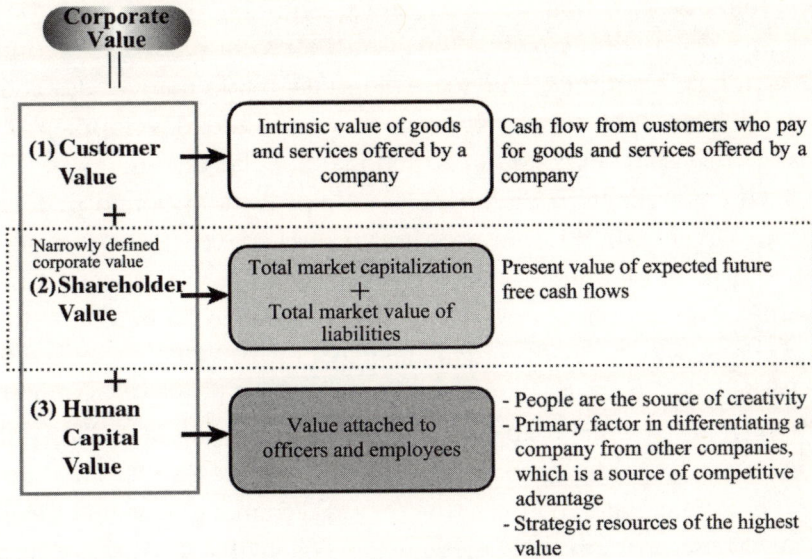

Corporate Value

(1) Customer Value

Intrinsic value of goods and services offered by a company

Cash flow from customers who pay for goods and services offered by a company

+

Narrowly defined corporate value

(2) Shareholder Value

Total market capitalization + Total market value of liabilities

Present value of expected future free cash flows

+

(3) Human Capital Value

Value attached to officers and employees

- People are the source of creativity
- Primary factor in differentiating a company from other companies, which is a source of competitive advantage
- Strategic resources of the highest value

EXHIBIT 1.12   New Theory of Corporate Value

maximization of customer value should naturally be the greatest challenge in any management strategy.

Shareholder Value. In this book, I define "shareholder value" not as total market capitalization alone, but as the sum of the total market value of liabilities and total market capitalization. Therefore, shareholder value, as referred to in this book, possesses the same meaning as the common definition of "corporate value." Shareholder value is the present value of free cash flows expected to be received by the shareholders and creditors of a company in the future. It goes without saying that the price of the stock of a company is most closely related to increases in the shareholder value of that company. When asked what indicator is predominantly linked to the price of a stock, most people would probably say return on equity (ROE). This is natural because a higher ROE means that the return on shareholders' equity is also high.

In recent years, thanks to the large-scale corporate restructuring being implemented by many companies, corporate profits have been making a V-shaped recovery. However, the recent recovery in corporate earnings is not due to increases in sales, but in many cases is the result of lower personnel expenses, research and development expenses, and capital expenditures, among other efficiencies.

Such cost reduction often results in improved corporate performance and eventually ROE in the short run. However, there is a good chance that, in the medium- to long-run, the cost reduction will prevent the development of new products and even have a negative effect on earnings, which will eventually lead to a lower ROE.

Let us take another example. It is considered in most cases that a share buyback scheme is an effective tool in improving ROE. However, share buyback also involves a risk that it may decrease the ratio of net worth to total capital and make the financial foundation of a company fragile. Therefore, any management approach that focuses only on ROE, in other words, shareholder value, is not desirable if a company is to achieve a healthy growth as a going concern or raise its corporate value in a true sense.

Human Capital Value. Human capital value is the value attached to the officers and employees of a company, and it is considered an important component of corporate value.

During the era of the Southern Sung Dynasty in China, Xie Fangde (1226–1289) wrote seven volumes of textbooks as a study guide to prepare prospective officials for recruitment exams. Found in the *Code of Writing*, one of these seven volumes, are the following words:

A country can be built by a person and it can be ruined by a person.

What this means is that a country built by a person of excellence will cease to exist when a person of excellence is lost. This saying also applies to a business enterprise; without superior human capital that possess a penetrating sense of mission and a self-sacrificing spirit, as well as an ability to exercise strong leadership, no company will be able to prosper perpetually. I believe that people are the source of creativity and a primary factor in the differentiation of a company from other companies, which in turn is a source of competitive advantage for that company. By recruiting and nurturing superior human capital, raising their motivation, and effectively taking advantage of them, a company can achieve exceptional results.

In this sense, it may be said that human capital is the most valuable strategic resource. The term "human capital" has been employed quite frequently in recent years. In addition, the top management executives of many corporations are giving priority to the hiring, fostering, and maintaining of human capital, and have remarked that this is their greatest challenge. I think that these are very positive signs.

We are now entering into an age when we must attach the utmost importance to human capital to the same degree as or even to a higher degree than we do to financial capital.

These three values are mutually linked. For example, if a company can offer products that possess a high customer value, then sales and profits will increase and share price will also rise, which will in turn increase shareholder value. When shareholder value has been increased, the value of stock options will also rise, which will ultimately raise the morale among all officers and employees of the company. In addition, if the company successfully hires individuals that have high moral standards and advanced skills, then these individuals can contribute to the raising of customer value, eventually leading to an increase in shareholder value. It is apparent, then, that the creation of such a positive growth cycle will consequently lead to a significant jump in corporate value.

Since many of the companies within the SBI Group are Internet-based companies, we place our highest priority on adherence to the customer-centric principle. In this regard, we are committed to the continuous improvement of customer value. We maintain outstanding human capital and utilize various incentive schemes, which make it possible for us to do just that, with the belief that these efforts will lead to an increase in customer value. The increase in customer value will then generate a positive growth cycle, which in turn will bring about a huge jump in corporate value (see Exhibit 1.13).

With the creation of customer value as a foundation,
corporate value is generated and increases through a mutual linkage
with shareholder value and human capital value.

Shareholder
Value

Human Capital
Value

Increase in shareholder value

Increase in human capital value

Increases in sales
and profits

Improvement in
incentives

Offering of
products with high
customer value

Increase in customer value

Adherence to a customer-centric principle in all group businesses

Customer Value

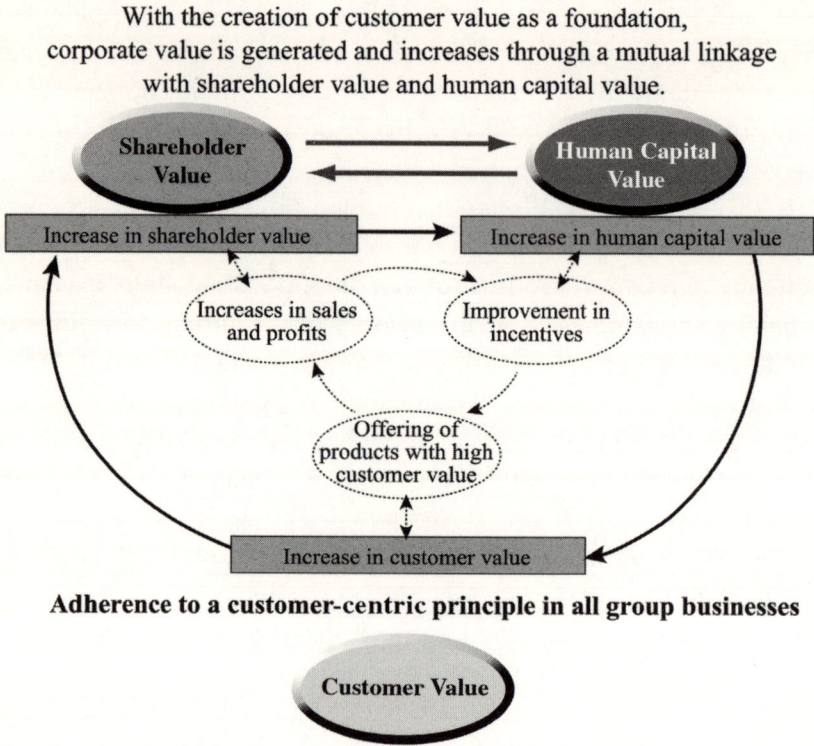

EXHIBIT 1.13   Mechanism for Raising Corporate Value

MANAGEMENT PHILOSOPHY OF THE SBI GROUP COMPANIES

Prior to the commencement of business, I decided to set forth a "management philosophy" for the SBI Group. I believe that any management philosophy usually takes the form of a "corporate mission," as in the United States. Each company normally establishes its own mission in a document that is called a "mission statement," which describes its corporate values and raison d'être.

A mission statement clearly defines the goals of a company and enables its employees to share a sense of purpose in working for the company.

While it appears that there are some management executives who consider such management philosophy to be nearly equivalent to a corporate vision, I make a clear distinction between the two concepts. A "corporate vision" concretely describes how a company sees itself in the future, and, therefore, it must be realistically valid and credible. On the other hand, I also believe that a corporate vision should be inspirational and capture the imagination of those involved.

Precisely because we live in a world of rapid changes and uncertainties, the leader of a nation or a corporation alike have the important role of presenting in a concrete manner an intriguing picture of what the nation or corporation will be like in the future; in other words, its vision. When a current leader steps down, such vision may be revised—or should be revised, in my own opinion—in accordance with the changes in circumstances or the prospect for such changes at that time.

In the present age of rapid change, a corporate vision is considered to be of a more medium-term nature, while a management philosophy is of a more long-term and universal nature and should not be changed easily because of shifts in top management or changes in various circumstances.

After having given careful consideration to these topics, I established the following five elements of management philosophy to be shared by all SBI Group companies (see Exhibit 1.14).

1. *To have sound ethical values* We shall undertake judgments on actions based not on whether they violate the law or profit the company, but on whether they are socially justifiable. In the book entitled *Zen of Vegetable Roots* (*Caigentan*), a collection of social teachings written by Hong Ying Ming during the era of the Ming Dynasty it is written, "Virtue is the foundation of a business." It means that a person's virtue is what forms the basis for driving his or her business to grow. Also, Peter Drucker once gave this profound comment: "Do the right things through people." Regardless of age and culture, the greatest importance is to have proper ethical values.

2. *To be a financial innovator* We shall bring superior innovations to the traditional roles of the financial industry, capitalize

on the incredible price-cutting power of the Internet, and through our customer-centric principle, create financial products and services to the further benefit of customers.

3. *To aim at becoming a new industry creator*   We shall become a leader who plays a major role in the creation and fostering of the core industries of the twenty-first century, primarily in knowledge-driven fields, such as the Internet and biotechnology fields.

4. *Continued self-evolution*   We shall continue to be a self-evolving company through the formation of an organization that flexibly adapts to the changes in the economic environment and through the integration of a corporate DNA composed of ingenuity and self-transformation into that organization.

5. *To fulfill social responsibilities*   We shall ensure that each company in the SBI Group fulfills its social and economic responsibilities to its stakeholders (interested parties) and society.

Five Elements of the

SBI Group's Management Philosophy

1. To Have Sound Ethical Values

2. To Be a Financial Innovator

3. To Aim at Becoming a New Industry Creator

4. To Carry Out Self-Evolution

5. To Fulfill Social Responsibility

EXHIBIT 1.14   Five Elements of the SBI Group's Management Philosophy

This management philosophy will be recognized by virtue of its raison d'être only when it is backed by a management strategy that is realistically valid in the course of corporate activities.

Three Fundamental Business Building Concepts

In a world where the previously mentioned Financial Big Bang and the Internet Revolution continue to progress in parallel, I determined that the following three concepts should be established as fundamental business building concepts. Allow me to explain them one by one.

Adherence to the Customer-Centric Principle

At SBI Group companies, it is my full belief that the customer-centric principle must always come first, no matter what the circumstances. What this principle entails is that we must provide services in exchange for the lowest commissions and interest rates possible, and that we offer compelling investment opportunities, one-list comparison of various financial products, highly secure and reliable services, and extensive, high quality financial content. Of course, there are a variety of other things that need to be covered, but we have been implementing various initiatives with our unchanged policy of putting customers first from the very beginning when the SBI Group was being established.

Integration of Online and Brick-and-Mortar Channels Based on the Customer-Centric Principle. While taking steps to ensure adherence to the customer-centric principle, I have begun to sense strongly that the integration of online and brick-and-mortar channels will have to inevitably occur. I believe that online channels alone cannot ensure adherence to the customer-centric principle, and neither can brick-and-mortar channels alone. Perhaps the customer-centric principle can be realized only through the integration of online and brick-and-mortar channels.

Customers come in all types. Some are able to use a PC and some are not. In adhering to the customer-centric principle, we cannot serve only those customers who have access to the Internet. Also, there are some customers who are able to adequately assess risks on their own, while others need to be given an adequate explanation of such risks, as the Internet alone cannot fully explain all such risks. Therefore, I feel that adherence to the customer-centric principle is possible only through the integration of both on and offline channels.

The "Winners" among U.S. Internet-Based Companies. The collapse of the U.S. Internet bubble in the spring of 2000 was followed by a period during which it became fairly clear that Internet-based companies were divided into so-called "winners" and "losers." A careful observation of the various companies in the winners column reveals that each and every one has adhered to the customer-centric principle.

How do the big three U.S. Internet-based companies (i.e., Yahoo!, Amazon.com, and eBay) compare to other companies in the same industry in terms of the level of customer satisfaction? According to the customer satisfaction ratings released by the American Customer Satisfaction Index (ACSI), as expected, the winners, especially those that ranked first, scored very high in terms of customer satisfaction. Yahoo! ranked first with a score of 76, in the portal category, Amazon.com ranked first with a score of 87 in the e-commerce category, followed by eBay ranking first with a score of 81 in the auction category (see Exhibit 1.15).

These ratings suggest that even though the companies may provide the same type of services, the companies with the highest level of customer satisfaction have become the leaders among the winners.

Moreover, the CEOs or executive managers of these companies have continuously expressed the importance of valuing their customers. For example, Jeff Bezos, the chairman of Amazon.com, Inc., has repeatedly said, "Customers are always right"; "I want to make our company the most customer-oriented company in the history of the world"; and "Increasing customer value is more important than anything else."

eBay Inc. has also expressed that it must "emphasize a sense of trust among its users" and that the company "values its community of users." In 2006, there were as many as 180 million registered users on eBay, and

(Maximum score for customer satisfaction: 100)

Portal	Second quarter 2006
Yahoo! Inc.	**76**
America Online, Inc. (Time Warner Inc.)	74
MSN (Microsoft Corporation)	74

E-Commerce (Retail)	Fourth quarter 2006
Amazon.com, Inc.	**87**
barnesandnoble.com Inc.	87
BUY.COM Inc.	80

E-Commerce (Auction)	Fourth quarter 2006
eBay Inc.	**81**
uBid, Inc.	73
priceline.com Inc.	72

EXHIBIT 1.15   The Big Three U.S. Internet-based Companies That Scored High in a Customer Satisfaction Survey
Source: American Customer Satisfaction Index (ACSI).

in the same year, the company recorded 1.9 billion listings from which it earned its revenues. It is therefore clear that eBay must give priority to its customers. Likewise, Yahoo! Inc. has continuously made comments such as, "Since we hold various types of information, we must undertake exhaustive efforts to protect customer information," as well as, "We must maintain a neutral position when providing information."

DEVELOPMENT OF STRUCTURAL DIFFERENTIATION

I believe that competition in the age of the Internet is completely different in nature from the previous form of competition, that is, competition prior to the emergence of the Internet. Then it was competition between an individual company against another individual company.

In other words, the various individual companies attempted to survive competition through the differentiation of prices, service quality, and product diversity. However, the age of the Internet has transformed this form of competition into a network-to-network competition.

In this new form of competition, it has become increasingly important for companies to develop a "structural differentiation" (see Exhibit 1.16).

Structural differentiation is a winning factor that enables a company to realize an unparalleled differentiation in order to prevent others from keeping pace with the company in a cutthroat and fierce competition within the age of the Internet. It may also be considered the pillar of the competitive strategy of that company.

In Sun Tzu's *Art of War* are the words:

Now the general who wins a battle makes many calculations in his temple ere the battle is fought.

This means that the person who wins a battle has a profoundly diverse variety of plans prepared beforehand, while the person who loses has not. Therefore, it is easy to see beforehand who is likely to

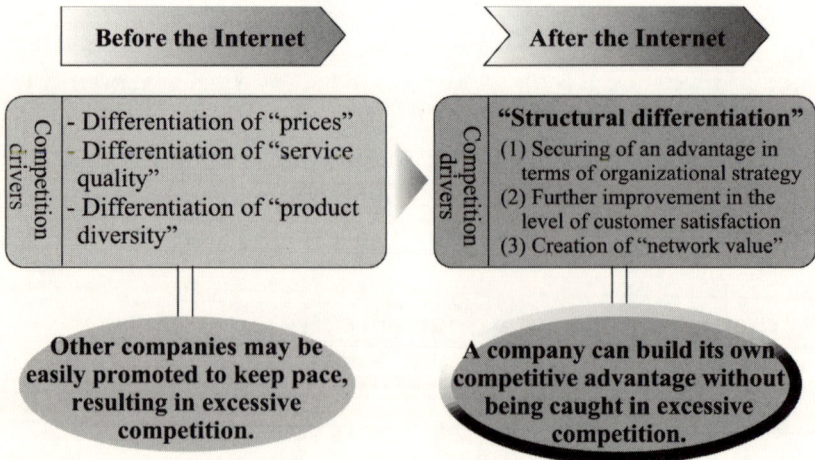

EXHIBIT 1.16   Age of the Internet and Structural Differentiation

win or lose a battle. This saying explains exactly why I have consciously built various structural differentiation tools into each group company since its establishment. As a result, these built-in differentiation tools always start to take effect at a certain point and ultimately help drive competitors away.

COMPREHENSIVE SUPPORT SYSTEM: THE SBI GROUP TAKES CARE OF EVERY CUSTOMER

Let us now look at an example of structural differentiation. I founded the company Softbank Investment Corporation (currently SBI Holdings, Inc.) and began a venture capital business. Since the idea of venture capital is to assist each venture firm in going public (IPO), it needs assistance from a securities firm when realizing an IPO. Therefore, E*Trade Securities Co., Ltd., (currently SBI E*TRADE SECURITIES Co., Ltd.) can act as an agent and an underwriter. However, in a number of cases, even after venture capital provides an equity investment in a venture firm, there still remains a substantial amount of funds to be raised before an IPO actually takes place.

In such cases, Softbank Frontier Securities Co., Ltd. (currently SBI Securities Co., Ltd.) can step in to procure the required funding. By creating a business model that involves Softbank Frontier Securities in such a manner (I have actually obtained a patent on this model), I made it possible for venture firms to engage in a second and even third round of fundraising prior to an IPO (see Exhibit 1.17). Maintaining such continuity provides a tool for the constant recycling of cash within the group without any part of it flowing outside.

Basically, the idea here is that we will not allow our competitors to take any of our customers from us and that the SBI Group companies will take care of all of their needs. The building of a comprehensive support system such as that described here is quite common in structural differentiation.

Structure That Ensures No Consolidated Losses. Another example is E*Trade. When I created the E*Trade Group, I established E*Trade Japan K.K.,

Building of a Comprehensive IPO Underwriting System

SBI Securities

SBI Investment

Providing support for the growth of venture firms

Underwriting

Subscription and sale

||

Venture firms

Approx. 400 firms

Providing a market for private equity issuance and distribution

IPO

Individual investors

Newly listed shares

Underwriting

Subscription and sale

SBI E*TRADE SECURITIES

IPO Securities Ltd.

Assessing securities issued by private firms, and guidance on the preparation of disclosure data

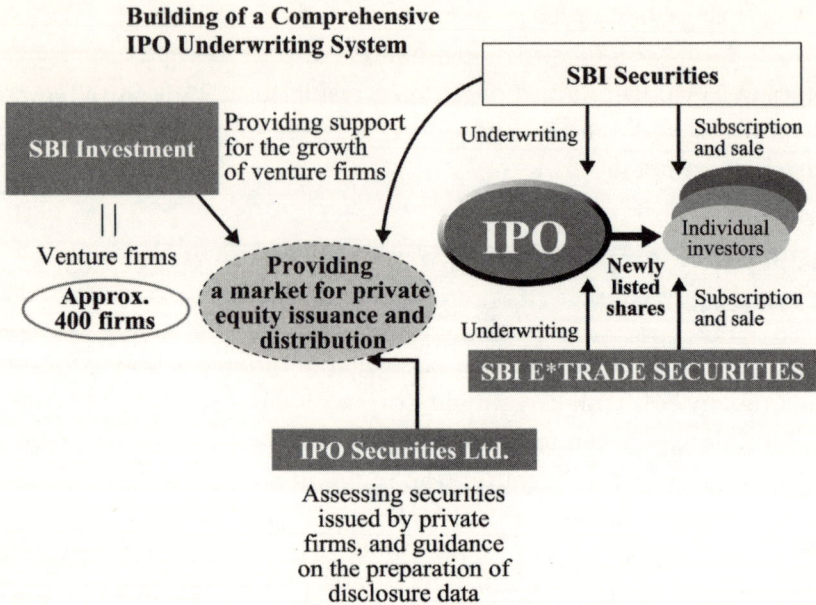

EXHIBIT 1.17   Example of Structural Differentiation (1)

and E*Trade Securities Co., Ltd. as a wholly owned subsidiary of the former. At that time, no other online securities firm, such as Matsui Securities or DLJ Direct SFG Securities (currently Rakuten Securities), was controlled by a holding company or a parent company.

Let me explain why I decided to structure the E*Trade Group as I did. Around that time, when I was launching E*Trade Securities in Japan, I checked the situation in the United States and found that there were already some 90 companies that were engaged in fierce competition to cut brokerage commissions. It truly was cutthroat competition.

When I saw what was happening in the United States, where online brokers were engaged in cutthroat competition by dramatically lowering their commission rates, I decided to create E*Trade Japan K.K., and I was not going to make this company a regular securities firm, but rather a company that would be able to undertake a variety of things to the extent allowed it by its articles of incorporation. Another thing I decided was that E*Trade Japan would have a double-layered structure, with various very profitable companies under its umbrella, since the plan for E*Trade Japan was to eventually go public, profitability would be very important (see Exhibit 1.18).

Therefore, I was determined to create a structure under which no losses would be reported on a consolidated basis. Under this structure, even if E*Trade Securities were to report a loss as a result of offering the lowest brokerage commissions in the industry, the loss could be offset by profits generated by other consolidated group companies, and thus no consolidated loss was reported. Fortunately, E*Trade Securities began to generate profits in its early days, and so in retrospect, I did not need to worry as much as I had. Nonetheless, through this exercise I gained a very positive experience, and the decision to use the

Double-layer structure strategy of E*Trade
(before the merger of E*Trade Japan K.K. and SBI)

All subsidiaries of E*Trade Japan K.K., with the exception of E*Trade Securities, will strive to increase earnings through the development of diversified businesses without being constrained by the regulations governing the securities industry, while E*Trade Japan K.K., a listed company, will maintain stable earnings on a consolidated basis. E*Trade Securities, on the other hand, will seek, regardless of its operating results, to offer the lowest commission schedule in the industry and work to expand its business with a competitive advantage.

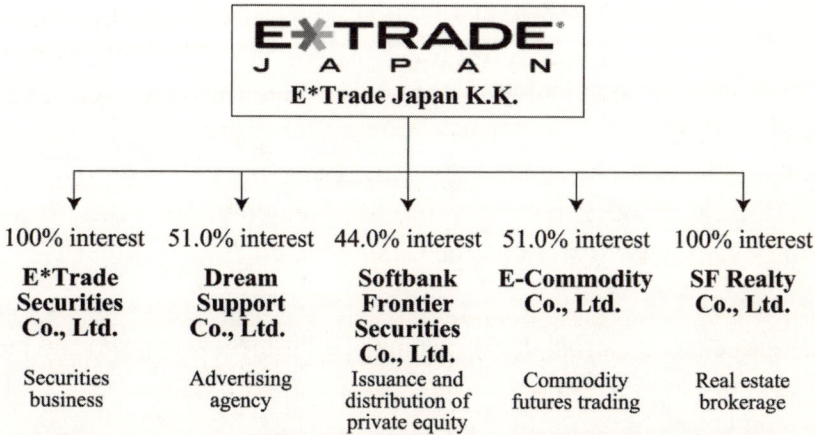

E✱TRADE
J A P A N
E*Trade Japan K.K.

100% interest	51.0% interest	44.0% interest	51.0% interest	100% interest
E*Trade Securities Co., Ltd.	**Dream Support Co., Ltd.**	**Softbank Frontier Securities Co., Ltd.**	**E-Commodity Co., Ltd.**	**SF Realty Co., Ltd.**
Securities business	Advertising agency	Issuance and distribution of private equity	Commodity futures trading	Real estate brokerage

EXHIBIT 1.18   Example of Structural Differentiation (2)

double-layered structure was a good one, as it would likely benefit the group in terms of its future strategies.

This, then, is the reason why I was eventually able to merge E*Trade Japan with Softbank Investment. In addition, E*Trade Securities, which became a wholly owned subsidiary of the new Softbank Investment as a result of the merger, was also successful in going public in 2004 (see Exhibit 1.19).

E*Trade Securities was a company that had never publicly offered its shares before. At that time, E*Trade Japan, a listed company, operated as a systems provider to E*Trade Securities and was also an operating holding company with various subsidiaries under its supervision. When E*Trade Securities went public, some argued that the company was actually going public for the second time. That argument is incorrect. E*Trade Securities has gone public only once and never prior to that point. I also call this case another example of structural differentiation.

This type of structural differentiation is considered strategically important in the United States as well. I mention the case of eBay and PayPal as an example.

In October 2002, eBay acquired PayPal, a company that provides online payment services. They began to incorporate the online settlement features of PayPal into the eBay platform, with the intention of providing these features to eBay users. Through this initiative, eBay was now able to offer improved convenience to its users. In addition, with PayPal as its subsidiary, eBay could expect the operating results of PayPal to grow, which would in turn contribute to better consolidated results.

From the point of view of eBay, the company was able to have its cake and eat it, too. A new structure was created through this process; this is what I refer to as structural differentiation.

Synergies Generated from the Formation of a Business Ecosystem and the Creation of a Network Value

About a half year into 1998, I started to study diversified companies with a particular focus on conglomerates. At the same time, while

**Development process for stand-alone public offering by
E*Trade Securities Co., Ltd.**

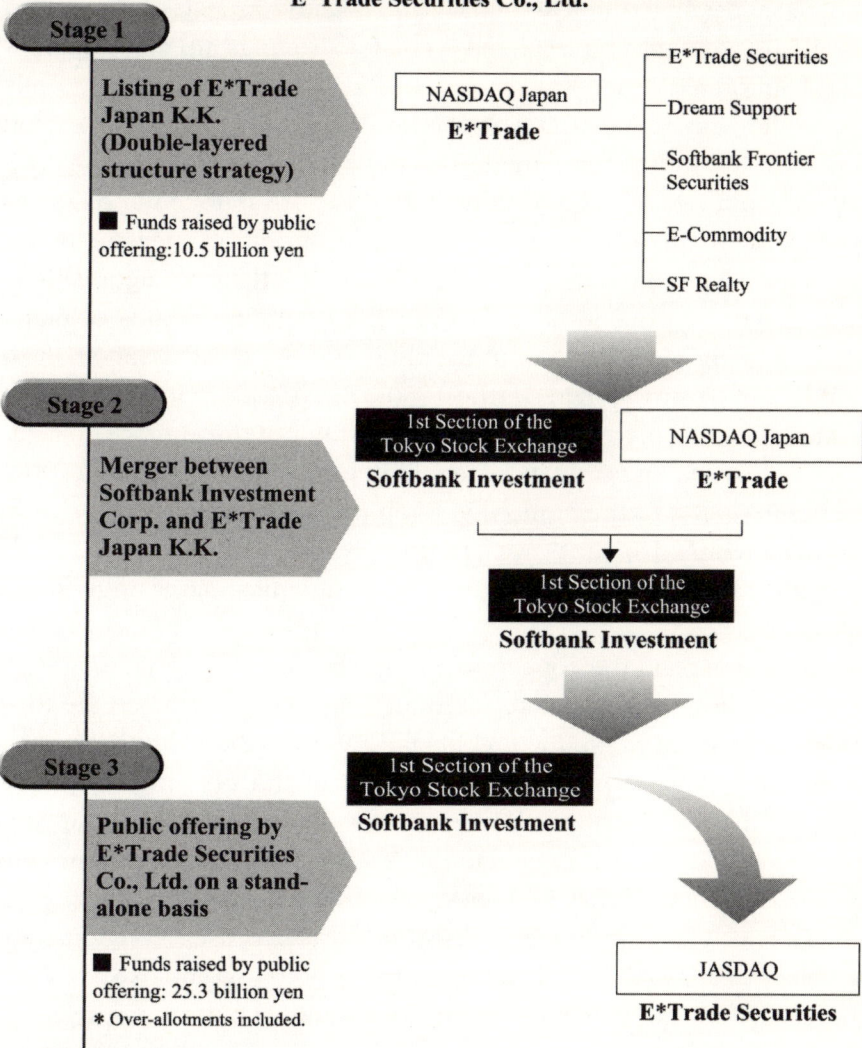

Stage 1

**Listing of E*Trade
Japan K.K.
(Double-layered
structure strategy)**

■ Funds raised by public
offering:10.5 billion yen

NASDAQ Japan
E*Trade

─ E*Trade Securities

─ Dream Support

─ Softbank Frontier
Securities

─ E-Commodity

─ SF Realty

Stage 2

**Merger between
Softbank Investment
Corp. and E*Trade
Japan K.K.**

1st Section of the
Tokyo Stock Exchange
Softbank Investment

NASDAQ Japan
E*Trade

1st Section of the
Tokyo Stock Exchange
Softbank Investment

Stage 3

**Public offering by
E*Trade Securities
Co., Ltd. on a stand-
alone basis**

■ Funds raised by public
offering: 25.3 billion yen
* Over-allotments included.

1st Section of the
Tokyo Stock Exchange
Softbank Investment

JASDAQ
E*Trade Securities

EXHIBIT 1.19   Example of Structural Differentiation (3)

imagining that our group would one day manage a number of subsidiaries, I began to think about how the negative aspects of a so-called conglomerate could be removed so that a strong group of companies could be formed.

In the United States, it was not until conglomerates like Textron Inc. and ITT Industries emerged in the 1960s that the view that diversification could add additional value to corporate value began to spread. Subsequently, a number of large corporations became diversified by expanding their business domains through acquisitions and mergers. In the 1980s, however, the operating results of many of these conglomerates began to falter, and the trend of diversification began to slow down. In the 1990s, the popular view was that a company could increase its corporate value not through diversification, but by leaving only its core competencies and spinning off the remaining parts of the company. Even in the stock market, the term "conglomerate discount" was frequently employed, and investors began to find investment in pure-play companies increasingly more appealing.

Let me explain the concept of conglomerate discount in a little bit more detail. A "conglomerate discount" is said to exist when the total business value of the individual business entities that comprise a conglomerate, which is a simple summation of the potential corporate value of the individual business entities, is larger than the overall corporate value of the conglomerate (in general, this difference ranges between 15 percent and 20 percent).

The need to identify such a discount exists because a conglomerate is created based on a fundamental proposition in complexity science that states "a mass, which is composed of multiple parts, must be larger than the aggregate of the multiple parts."

Why, then, is such a discount generated? The main reason, as pointed out by economists, is "diseconomies of scope," which results from the difficulty of managing multiple businesses. It is not very often that we find super management executives who are able to manage a number of business entities. A mediocre management executive will find it hard to manage a company after it has been conglomeratized, and synergies may not be effectively created between the various business entities of that company. As a result, the company will end up a mere combination of unsynchronized separate entities, with a management who lacks the decision-making speed and alacrity.

To demonstrate how bond rating agencies view this issue, I cite some of the statements made in a report released by Standard & Poor's (S&P), a leading rating agency. S&P states,

> The establishment of a holding company is only a management technique, and this alone does not have any impact on ratings. The important thing is how to effectively make use of a holding company.

However, in general,

> The counter-party rating of a holding company cannot be higher than the rating of its subsidiary. If the subsidiary has an investment grade rating, then the counter-party rating of the holding company will be rated at least one notch below that investment grade rating. If the subsidiary has a non-investment grade rating, then the holding company's counter-party rating will be at least two notches below the former. The above criteria reflect a structural subordination of the creditors of a parent company to the creditors of its subsidiary.

This structural subordination is defined as follows:

- The financial claims of the creditors of a parent company are subordinated to the financial claims of the creditors of its subsidiary.
- When a majority of operating assets are present in a subsidiary and the subsidiary is being wound up, the creditors of its parent company are subordinated to the creditors of the subsidiary excluding the case that the creditors of the parent company hold security rights on the assets of the subsidiary.

S&P further states in the same report that the following points have an impact on ratings:

- Whether the holding company concerned is a pure holding company or an operating holding company.
- The level and stability of the dividends received from subsidiaries of the holding company concerned.
- The amount of liabilities of the holding company concerned, their maturity dates, and payment schedule; liquidity and quality of assets; and level of capital.
- Management control structure and compliance.
- Whether it is necessary to support subsidiaries.

S&P says that, even with these points taken into consideration, "in the light of the structurally subordinated nature of a holding company noted earlier, it is extremely unusual for a holding company and its subsidiary to possess the same rating, although such case is not entirely nonexistent."

Even though the rating of bonds is an entirely different matter from that of the assessment of stocks, I include this information for reference purposes.

Given the information such as that just described, I examined from various angles the pros and cons of creating a corporate group. As long as the group remained a subsidiary of Softbank Finance, which is a wholly owned subsidiary of SOFTBANK CORP., the diversification of the group would have some kind of impact, be it positive or negative, on the profit and loss statement of SOFTBANK. If the impact was substantially negative, then SOFTBANK would suffer greatly. Therefore, it was necessary to create a structure that would avoid any negative impact on SOFTBANK as much as possible. I kept thinking that the creation of such structure would ultimately strengthen the overall SOFTBANK Group, and, therefore, the group would not necessarily be subjected to a "conglomerate discount." It is based on this thought that I came up with the following ideas:

- Each new company to be established would start generating profits as soon as possible.

- Each subsidiary within the group would become successful enough to be able to make a public offering as soon as possible, after which time it would be spun off from the group. Once the subsidiary became publicly held, it would exploit its own fundraising capacity as an autonomous and independent company and strive for self-growth without the creation of any financial burden on the parent company.

- Each subsidiary within the group must be strongly aware that it was a member of an economic community. Therefore, it would be necessary to create a collective corporate entity that allowed for mutual synergies to be generated between the various subsidiaries.

- This economic community would continuously maintain and enhance a strong sense of solidarity or bond within the group through the capital relationships between the parent and subsidiaries, the synergies generated between the group companies, common values and vision, and the strategies shared by the group companies, the various personal relationships within the group, the corporate culture, and so on.

- Not only the parent company, but each subsidiary would hold on to the spirit of a venture capitalist on a permanent basis, devote their entire attention to speedy management, and strive to keep up its "business metabolism" in order to avoid succumbing to the so-called "big-business syndrome." That is, each group company would consistently identify and cultivate the growth potential within itself, while spinning off any business that had placed itself on a growth track and allowing it to self-grow as an independent company.

This strategy is very important as a company needs to select and concentrate on its core competencies in the age of the Internet. The Internet has dramatically broadened the span of control of a company and has increased the number of its customers, suppliers, partners, competitors,and so on, as well as increased the complications in the relationships between them. For example, a company will likely see its local customer and supplier base expand not only within, but beyond Japan. When this occurs, the company will not be able to control everything on its own and will be forced to select and concentrate on its core competencies.

- All companies within the group would be Internet-based companies, a majority of which would provide financial services. Therefore, from a groupwide point of view, the group of companies to be created would offer one-stop convenience for customers to fulfill every possible financial need. However, it would be completely meaningless for the group companies to function in an unsynchronized manner alone, even if the group were to cover every area of financial service. It would be very important to have all group companies form a single complete network and create mutually beneficial partnerships among them. Also important would be to have the group companies mutually make use of their customer bases in order to realize a cross-selling of products, as well as share their respective networks and partnerships with nongroup companies.

While pondering these ideas and reading a number of books and scholarly articles, I came across some very encouraging studies authored by two scholars.

Degree of Relatedness among Multiple Business Entities and Business Performance

Categories of Relatedness. One of the studies was detailed in the Japanese translation of the book entitled *Takakuka Senryaku to Keizai Seika* (*Strategy, Structure, and Economic Performance* by Richard P. Rumelt (translated by Kinichiro Toba et al., Toyo Keizai Inc., Tokyo, 1977). The book describes a study on the relationship between the degree of relatedness among multiple business entities and the overall business performance of the company that is comprised by these entities.

In the book, Rumelt classifies businesses into three categories by relatedness: dominant business firms, related business firms, and unrelated business firms (see Exhibit 1.20).

The related business firm category refers to a company that does not have a single primary business, but has a business portfolio that has a consistent relatedness among the various businesses that comprise the portfolio. The unrelated business firm category includes a type of company typically described as a diversified conglomerate that has practically no relatedness among the various businesses that comprise the company. The conclusion of this study is that a company whose business portfolio has a higher relatedness tends to have a higher profitability. I was very encouraged by this conclusion, as it backed up my own intuition that if the synergetic effect among related business entities works, we should see higher earnings as a result.

Does business diversification create a positive impact on business results?

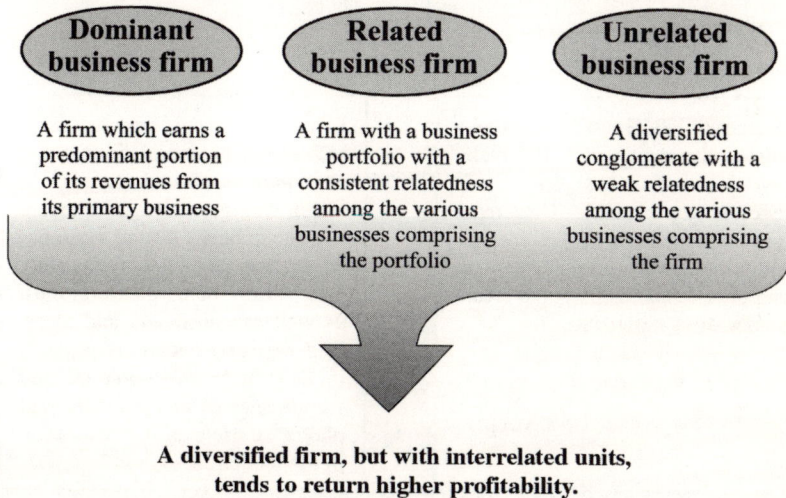

Dominant business firm	**Related business firm**	**Unrelated business firm**
A firm which earns a predominant portion of its revenues from its primary business	A firm with a business portfolio with a consistent relatedness among the various businesses comprising the portfolio	A diversified conglomerate with a weak relatedness among the various businesses comprising the firm

A diversified firm, but with interrelated units, tends to return higher profitability.

EXHIBIT 1.20   Logical Base for the SBI Group's Business Ecosystem (1)
Source: Strategy, Structure, and Economic Performance by Richard P. Rumelt (Toyo Keizai Inc., Tokyo, 1977).

The Business Ecosystem Concept. The other study consists of two essays authored by U.S. scholar James F. Moore published in the *Harvard Business Review* in 1993, entitled "Predators and Prey: A New Ecology of Competition" and "The Death of Competition: Leadership and Strategy in the Age of Business Ecosystems" (HarperBusiness, New York, 1996).

In his essays, Moore clearly sets forth the concept of a "business ecosystem" and argues how important it is to implement this concept in corporate management (see Exhibit 1.21).

I then realized that this concept of a "business ecosystem" is essentially the same as the ideal image of a corporate group that I had been vaguely envisioning. I found very excellent ideas in these essays. For example:

> Successful businesses are those that evolve rapidly and effectively. Yet, innovative businesses can't evolve in a vacuum. They must attract resources of all sorts, drawing in capital, partners, suppliers, and customers to create cooperative networks.

This paragraph genuinely expresses the need for a business ecosystem. Further:

Successful businesses are those that evolve rapidly and effectively. Yet innovative businesses can't evolve in a vacuum. They must attract resources of all sorts, drawing in capital, partners, suppliers, and customers to create cooperative networks.	In an age of rapid and full-scale technological innovations . . . managers need to have a clear vision and a strong will to create a new concept of a "business ecosystem," with the involvement of a variety of corporate groups, as well as consumers and users, lead as many people as possible to believe in the potential and significance of such a model, and play a key role in the realization of the model.

EXHIBIT 1.21   Logical Base for the SBI Group's Business Ecosystem (2)
Source: The Death of Competition: Leadership and Strategy in the Age of Business Ecosystems by James F. Moore (HarperBusiness, New York, 1993).

In the age of rapid and full-scale technological innovations, the traditional concept of competition against peers loses its significance. Rather than engaging in competition on the strength of a certain product or make a company successful, managers today need to have a clear vision and a strong will to create a new concept of a "business ecosystem" with the involvement of a variety of corporate groups, as well as consumers and users, lead as many people as possible to believe in the potential and significance of such a model, and play a key role in the realization of the model.

It really struck home to me when I read this, for it describes exactly what I had been thinking about, and I was ever motivated. In this sense, I was able to gain an unwavering will and commitment to follow this concept of a business ecosystem, while working to create a group that would allow synergetic effects to proficiently materialize within itself.

I believe that any management strategy and management policy must be underpinned by sound logic. It is very important for management executives to thoroughly understand such logic. I am pretty sure that there are not many who would follow an order to do something without being given a clear logic or reason for doing it. That is why I believe that it is imperative to always be clear as to why something is being done.

There are some who take little account of academic achievements when it comes to management. These people would often say that there is no place for academics in the business world. Academic achievements are only ideas thought up by scholars. However, I believe that even when it comes to management, clear reasons and logical proof are a necessity. For example, Adam Smith wrote *The Wealth of Nations*, which became the spirit behind the lower middle class who rose to power at that time, and it helped press forward the Industrial Revolution. Without some sort of bible, I doubt if a revolution would have come about that easily. This is why I maintain the unfailing stance of properly incorporating academic achievements into the revolution I have been envisioning.

The idea of a business ecosystem is attributed to a concept that has been debated in the study of "complexity science" (see Exhibit 1.22). A

The two main propositions in "complexity" science

A mass, which is composed of multiple parts, must be larger than the aggregate of the multiple parts

A mass contains new characteristics that cannot be found in the multiple parts that comprise the mass

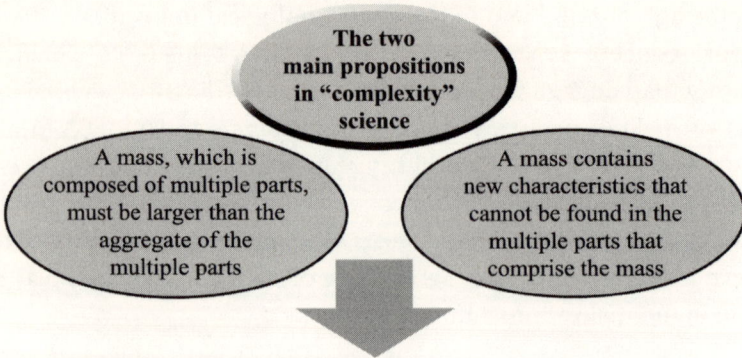

A business ecosystem, a new form of organization, should be developed in order to realize a high growth potential through a synergistic effect and mutual evolution among the various members of the ecosystem that cannot be accomplished by a stand-alone company.

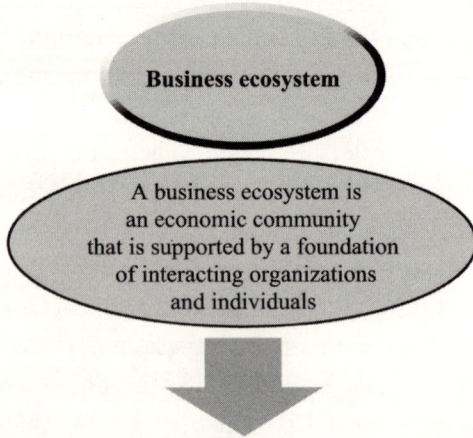

Business ecosystem

A business ecosystem is an economic community that is supported by a foundation of interacting organizations and individuals

In a business ecosystem, a company is not just a member of a single industry. Rather, a company becomes a part of a business ecosystem that extends over a wide range of industries, and it must work to realize a synergistic effect and mutual growth among the various members of the ecosystem.

EXHIBIT 1.22   Idea of an Organization Based on Knowledge of Complexity

"business ecosystem" is an economic community that is supported by a foundation of interacting organizations and individuals.

I became confident that a company could greatly enhance its growth potential by forming such a business ecosystem and creating positive mutual interfaces between group companies or groups.

The potential growth of a company viewed as a single economic entity is fairly limited, but a company is able to achieve a dramatic growth through forming and nurturing a business ecosystem, enabling the various business entities that comprise that ecosystem to mutually generate positive synergies among themselves, and mutually evolving with each of the markets in which the business entities operate (see Exhibit 1.23).

In addition, a company viewed as a single economic entity tends to

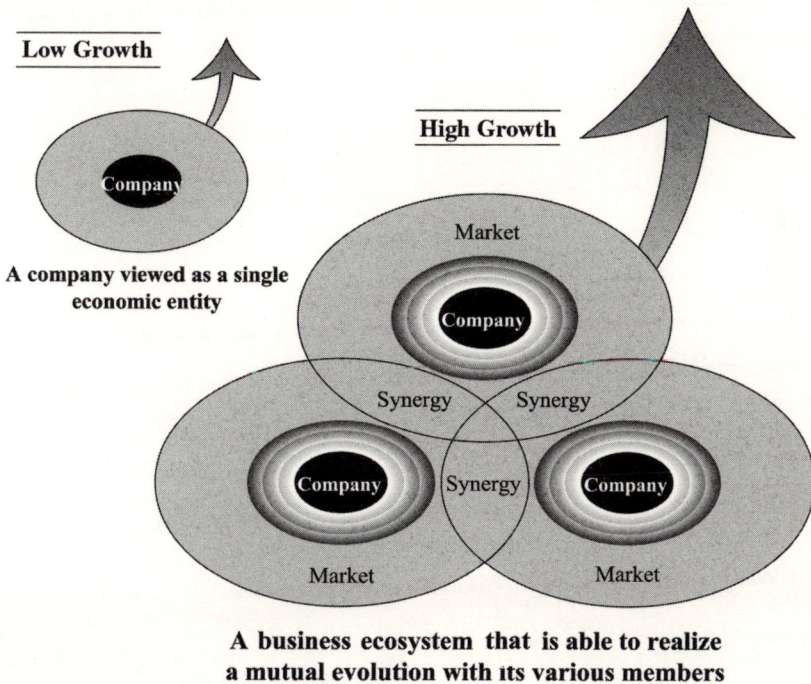

Low Growth

Company

A company viewed as a single economic entity

High Growth

Market

Company

Synergy   Synergy

Synergy

Company   Company

Market   Market

A business ecosystem that is able to realize a mutual evolution with its various members

EXHIBIT 1.23 Dramatic Corporate Growth through the Formation of a Business Ecosystem

have a low level of resistance to economic downturns, but a company that forms a business ecosystem, on the other hand, has a very high level of resistance to economic downturns. The idea here is that even if some members of the system succumb to a recession and suffer losses, the other surviving members are able to help the suffering members.

Perhaps the only way for us to demonstrate a network value appeal to customers is through the formation and nurturing of a business ecosystem and creating partnerships with other companies and group companies, as well as having them become involved in the system.

CHAPTER 2

The History and Deepening of the SBI Group's Organizational Strategy

NUMERICAL MEASUREMENT OF BUSINESS EXPANSION

Rapidly Changing Environment as the Driver of Dramatic Growth

The Internet Revolution has progressed at a speed that has been much faster than any of us could have imagined. According to the White Paper on the Internet (2005), the number of Internet users in Japan increased from 5,718,000 in February 1997 to 70,072,000 in February 2005, nearly 12.3 times. The number of users is nearly 3.8 times what it was five years ago in February 2000 when we launched the Internet Technology Fund (see Exhibit 2.1).

The number of broadband Internet users is also growing very rapidly. As of February 2005, the number of broadband Internet users reached approximately 32,240,000, which is nearly 5.5 times the number of users three years prior (see Exhibit 2.2). The rate of penetration has increased to 36.2 percent, which translates to more than one-third of all households in Japan.

With respect to electronic commerce, the *Survey on Actual Condition and Market Size of Electronic Commerce for 2004* (Information Economy

* From February 2004 onward, the number of users
include users aged three and older.

(10,000 users)

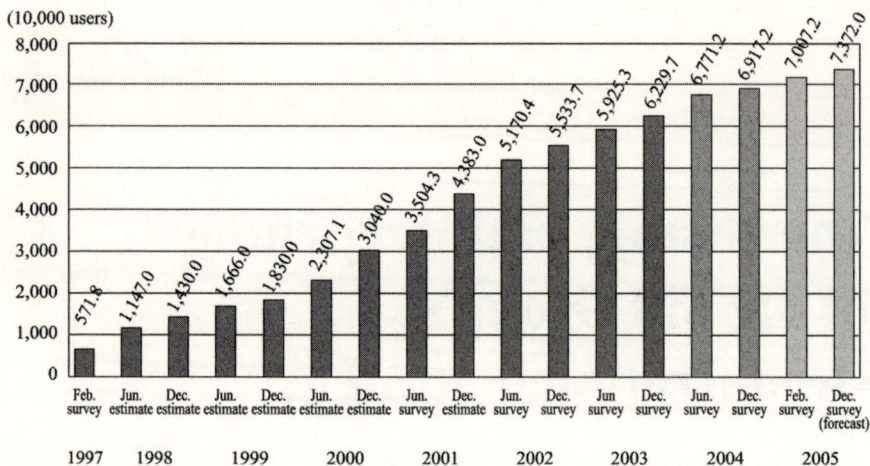

EXHIBIT 2.1 Changes in the Number of Internet Users in Japan
Source: 2005 White Paper on the Internet © Access Media/Impress, 2005.

(2002 to 2005) * From February 2004 onward, the number of
users include users aged three and older.

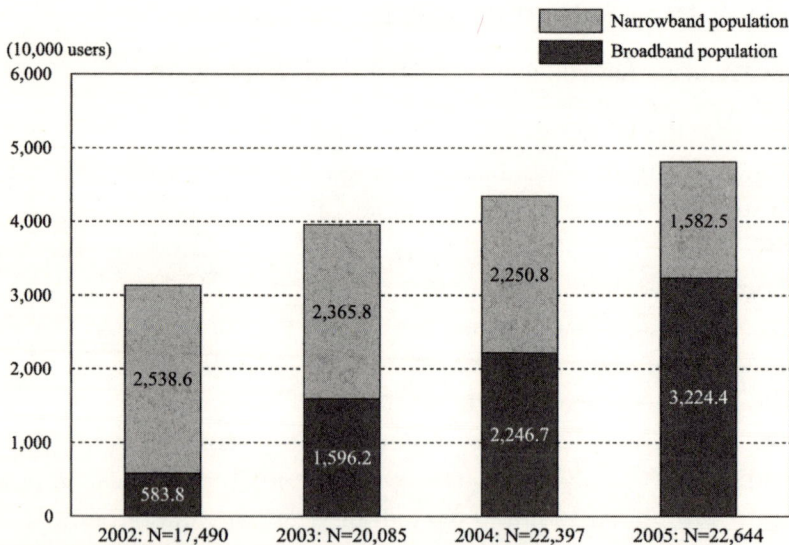

Note: The number of users in households using the Internet excluding those Internet users who have
access through "mobile phone/PHS only" and at "work/school only."

EXHIBIT 2.2 Changes in the Number of Broadband and Narrowband Users
Source: 2005 White Paper on the Internet © Access Media/Impress, 2005.

Outlook, 2005) reported that the size of the business-to-consumer (BtoC) market in 2004 reached 5.643 trillion yen (an increase of 28 percent from the previous year) and the electronic commerce (EC) rate was 2.1 percent. The size of the business-to-business (BtoB) market steadily expanded to 102.699 trillion yen (an increase of 33 percent from the previous year), with the EC rate reaching 14.7 percent (see Exhibit 2.3). In addition, the total amount circulated in the consumer-to-consumer (CtoC) market through Internet auctions reached 784 billion yen.

Changes in the BtoC-EC Market Size

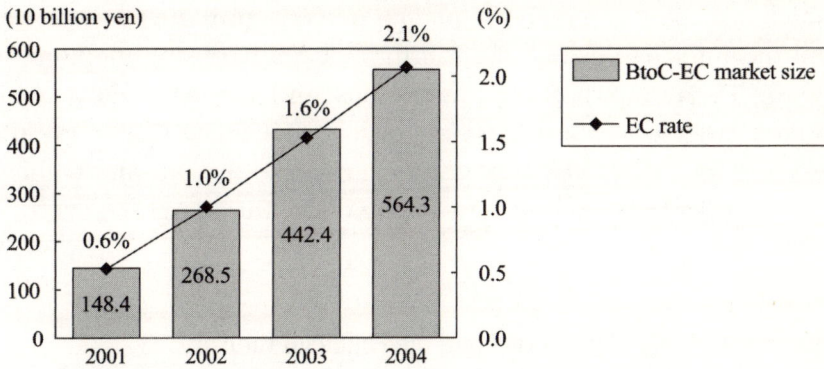

Changes in the BtoB-EC Market Size

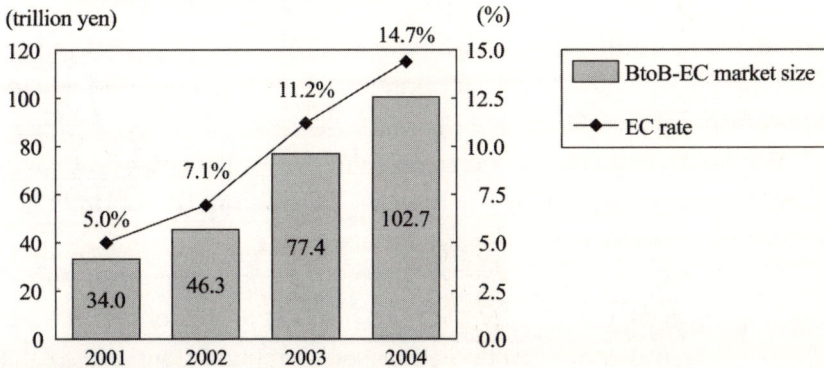

EXHIBIT 2.3   Changes in the BtoC and BtoB Markets in Japan

Sources: Survey on Actual Condition and Market Size of Electronic Commerce for 2004 (Information Economy Outlook 2005) jointly prepared by the Ministry of Economy, Trade and Industry (METI), the Next Generation Electronic Commerce Promotion Council of Japan (ECOM), and NTT Data Institute of Management Consulting, Inc.

A breakdown of BtoC transactions by the goods and services segment shows that the segment with the highest EC rate was the financial segment, which includes banks and securities firms, among others. In the other financial segment representing life and nonlife insurance, however, the EC rate was quite low at 0.4 percent. The segment for PC and related goods also showed a high EC rate of 16.6 percent (see Exhibit 2.4).

Internet advertising also grew in a large way. Expenditures were approximately 6.0 billion yen in 1997 and increased to 59.0 billion yen in 2000. Then, in 2005, the figure reached 280.8 billion yen, which represents an increase of 54.8 percent from the previous year, and the Internet became the fourth-largest advertising medium, following TV, newspapers, and magazines, and surpassed radio, which ranked last (see Exhibit 2.5). According to Dentsu Communication Institute Inc., there is a very good chance that the Internet will even surpass magazines in 2007 to become the third-largest advertising medium.

Interface between the Internet and the Financial Industry

As I outlined previously, the Internet market has grown remarkably since our group first made a foray into the Internet-based financial businesses in April 1999. Moreover, we should also note that in recent years the pace of growth has accelerated, driven by the rapid advancement of broadband.

The process of creative destruction in the past several years, which deserves to be looked at as the Internet Revolution, has brought about significant changes in every market that exists.

These changes had begun to occur first in the financial industry, which has the closest affinity with the Internet and later manifested itself in other industries. Anticipating such changes, our group made preemptive moves to aggressively expand into the Internet-based financial businesses. At that time, the existing major financial institutions were still plagued, in varying degrees, by the aftermath of the burst of the economic bubble formed during the 1980s, and they were far from

Goods and Services Segment	Previous Survey (2003)	
	Market Size (Yen)	EC Rate *1
PC and Related Goods	235.0 billion	16.0%
Travel	474.0 billion	3.4%
Entertainment *2	330.0 billion	2.8%
Books and Music *2	138.0 billion	4.4%
Clothing and Accessories	164.0 billion	1.3%
Food Products and Beverages	219.0 billion	0.5%
Hobbies, Miscellaneous Goods, and Furniture	249.0 billion	2.0%
Automobiles	603.0 billion	4.8%
Real Estate	912.0 billion	2.1%
Other Products	247.0 billion	1.0%
Financial	215.0 billion	0.7%
Financial (Banking, Securities, etc.)	146.0 billion	11.9%
Financial (Life and Non-Life Insurance)	69.0 billion	0.2%
Other Various Services	638.0 billion	0.8%
Total	4,424.0 billion	1.6%

Goods and Services Segment	Current Survey (2004)		
	Market Size (Yen)	EC Rate *1	Year-to-Year Comparison
PC and Related Goods	262.0 billion	16.6%	111.5%
Home Electrical Appliances *3	119.0 billion	1.8%	141.7%
Travel	661.0 billion	4.7%	139.5%
Entertainment *2	421.0 billion	3.5%	127.6%
Books and Music *2	207.0 billion	6.7%	150.0%
Clothing and Accessories	183.0 billion	1.4%	111.6%
Food Products and Beverages	299.0 billion	0.7%	136.5%
Medical, Cosmetic, and Health Food Products *3	222.0 billion	4.1%	144.2%
Hobbies, Miscellaneous Goods, Furniture, and Other *3	342.0 billion	1.3%	132.6%
Automobiles	656.0 billion	5.2%	108.8%
Real Estate	1,049.0 billion	2.4%	115.0%
Financial	321.0 billion	1.0%	149.3%
Financial (Banking, Securities, etc)	211.0 billion	16.8%	144.5%
Financial (Life and Non-Life Insurance)	110.0 billion	0.4%	159.4%
Other Various Services	901.0 billion	1.6%	141.2%
Total	5,643.0 billion	2.1%	127.6%

*1 The EC Rate is the ratio of the value of the EC market to the aggregate of final consumption, housing investments, and so on in the household sector.

*2 In 2004, the ChakuUta musical ringtone service was moved from the "Entertainment" segment to the "Books and Music" segment. The same applies to 2003.

*3 Beginning in the current survey, "Other Products" has been divided into a "Home Electrical Appliances" segment and a "Medical, Cosmetic, and Health Food Products" segment. The other goods and services (Other) have been included in the "Hobbies, Miscellaneous Goods, Furniture, and Other" segment.

EXHIBIT 2.4 EC Rates in the BtoC Market in Japan

Sources: Survey on Actual Condition and Market Size of Electronic Commerce for 2004 (Information Economy Outlook 2005) jointly prepared by the Ministry of Economy, Trade and Industry (METI), the Next Generation Electronic Commerce Promotion Council of Japan (ECOM), and NTT Data Institute of Management Consulting, Inc.

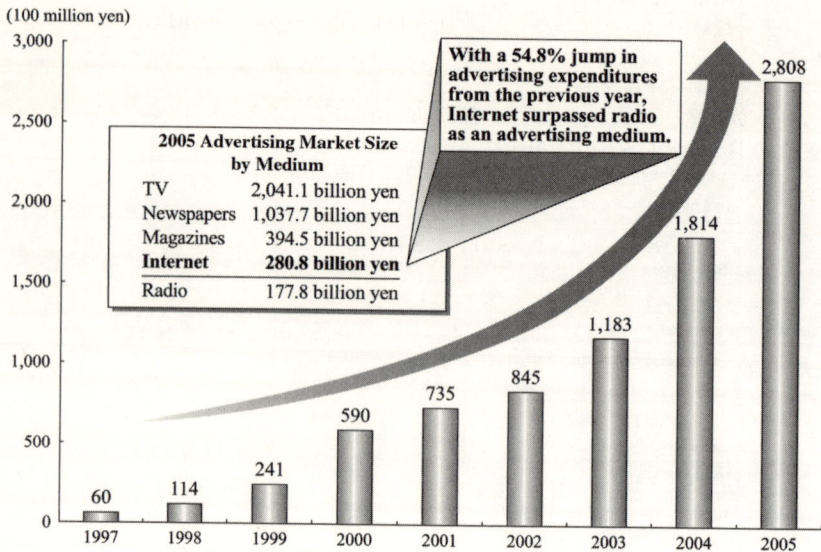

(100 million yen)

2005 Advertising Market Size by Medium

TV	2,041.1 billion yen
Newspapers	1,037.7 billion yen
Magazines	394.5 billion yen
Internet	**280.8 billion yen**
Radio	177.8 billion yen

With a 54.8% jump in advertising expenditures from the previous year, Internet surpassed radio as an advertising medium.

Year	Value
1997	60
1998	114
1999	241
2000	590
2001	735
2002	845
2003	1,183
2004	1,814
2005	2,808

EXHIBIT 2.5   Changes in Internet Advertising Expenditures in Japan
Source: 2005 Advertising Expenditures in Japan, Dentsu Communication.

considering undertaking a full-scale foray into Internet-based financial businesses.

By filling the space in the market left unattended by these financial institutions, we were able to form a group of companies as a business ecosystem in a relatively short period of time, particularly in the financial field where the advantage of the Internet was uniquely and fully utilized.

Tracing the SBI Group's Growth

Now let's look at how we have grown into the SBI Group, as it stands today, with reference to a few of our group companies as examples.

The Securities Industry and SBI E*TRADE.   The first example is SBI E*TRADE SECURITIES Co., Ltd. As was the case in the United States, the securities industry was subjected first and most significantly to the impact of the Internet Revolution. In October 1999, the securities industry welcomed the deregulation of stock brokerage commissions. A number of Internet pure-play securities firms opened for business as soon as the deregulation took effect, and the number of accounts quickly increased through the employment of low commissions as powerful ammunition.

The number of online transaction accounts, which had stood at 746,456 as of the end of March 2000, increased nearly 13.4 times to 10,003,099 by the end of March 2006 (see Exhibit 2.6). Backed by such a huge growth in the number of accounts, the ratio of Internet transactions to individual brokerage trading value grew to as high as 81 percent in the second half of 2005 (see Exhibit 2.7).

Shining in particular among the dramatic rise of the Internet pure-play securities firms was SBI E* TRADE SECURITIES. The company established a predominant position with respect to the number of accounts, share of individual brokerage trading value, and customers' assets in custody, which are the three most important indicators used in the evaluation of a securities firm.

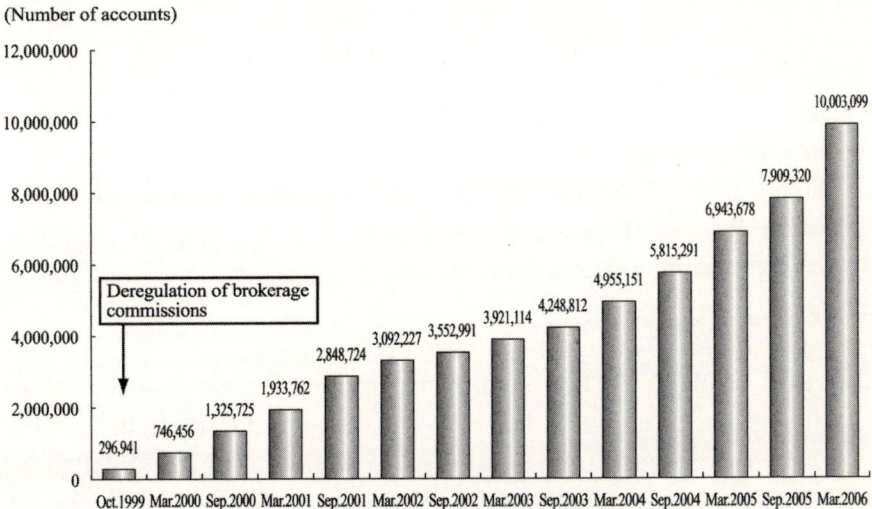

EXHIBIT 2.6 Rising Number of Online Transaction Accounts
Source: Results of Internet Transaction Survey (as of March 31, 2006), Japan Securities Dealers Association.

Individual brokerage
trading value
(trillion yen)

Ratio of online
transactions to the
individual brokerage
trading value   (%)

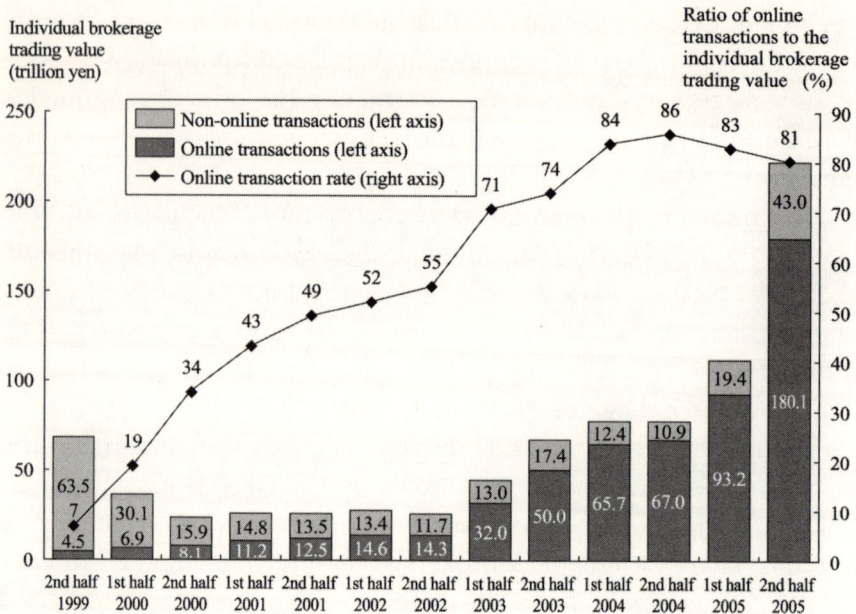

Legend:
- Non-online transactions (left axis)
- Online transactions (left axis)
- Online transaction rate (right axis)

Data points by half-year period:

Period	Online transactions	Non-online	Rate
2nd half 1999	4.5	63.5	7
1st half 2000	6.9	30.1	19
2nd half 2000	8.1	15.9	34
1st half 2001	11.2	14.8	43
2nd half 2001	12.5	13.5	49
1st half 2002	14.6	13.4	52
2nd half 2002	14.3	11.7	55
1st half 2003	32.0	13.0	71
2nd half 2003	50.0	17.4	74
1st half 2004	65.7	12.4	84
2nd half 2004	67.0	10.9	86
1st half 2005	93.2	19.4	83
2nd half 2005	180.1	43.0	81

EXHIBIT 2.7   Rapid Growth in the Ratio of Internet Transactions to the Individual
Brokerage Trading Value
Source: Results of Internet Transaction Survey, Japan Securities Dealers Association.

Such remarkable growth set SBI E*TRADE SECURITIES far apart from its competitors, and this gap continues to widen at an even faster pace. In terms of the share of individual brokerage trading value, SBI E*TRADE SECURITIES surpassed and gained a large lead over Nomura Securities, which has been a long-time industry leader (see Exhibits 2.8 and 2.9).

Marketplace and InsWeb. The marketplace business that our group offers has also grown along with the widespread use of the Internet.

Our marketplace business consists of services provided by the Ins-Web Division, the E-LOAN Division, and other divisions of Finance All Corporation (Finance All Corporation is now merged into SBI Holdings, Inc.). InsWeb offers consumers insurance related information and insurance quotes from various insurance companies participating in the

Nomura Securities' share in the total individual brokerage trading value was nearly 20 times that of SBI E*TRADE SECURITIES six years ago. In the fourth quarter of the fiscal year ending March 2006, SBI E*TRADE SECURITIES' share was now about 4.1 times that of Nomura Securities.

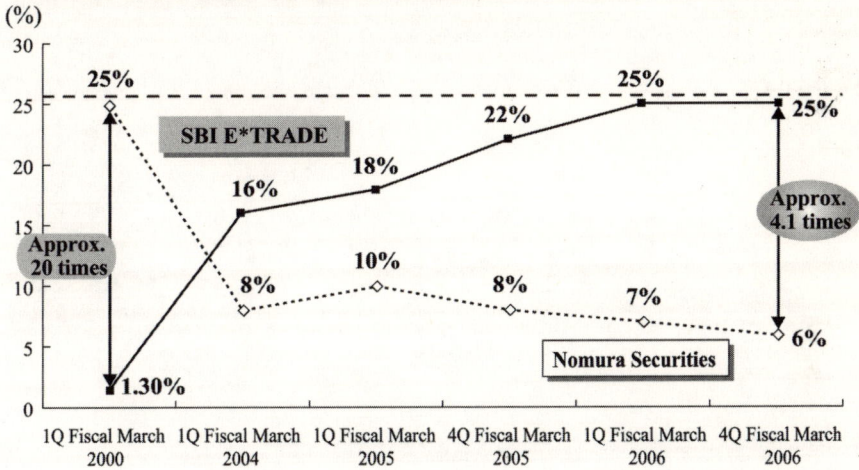

(%)

30

25%   25%   25%

SBI E*TRADE

18%

20

16%

Approx. 4.1 times

22%

15

Approx. 20 times

10%

10

8%   8%   7%

Nomura Securities

6%

5

1.30%

0

1Q Fiscal March 2000   1Q Fiscal March 2004   1Q Fiscal March 2005   4Q Fiscal March 2005   1Q Fiscal March 2006   4Q Fiscal March 2006

* SBI E*TRADE SECURITIES' share in the individual brokerage trading value is the sum of its shares on the three major markets, that is Tokyo, Osaka, and Nagoya Stock Exchanges (1st and 2nd sections), and JASDAQ.

EXHIBIT 2.8 Comparison of SBI E*TRADE SECURITIES with Nomura Securities in Terms of the Individual Brokerage Trading Value
Source: This information was compiled by the SBI Group based on statistical data provided by the Tokyo Stock Exchange and JASDAQ, as well as official data released on the web sites of Nomura Securities and SBI E*TRADE SECURITIES.

marketplace (where consumers can search and compare products) by providing them on the Internet, all free of charge.

Users of InsWeb can compare and study the various insurance services quoted by different insurance companies and purchase only those services that they wish to purchase. InsWeb utilizes a business model wherein it earns fees from participating insurance companies by linking them to potential customers who wish to obtain insurance quotes.

The business model employed by E-LOAN is, one might say, pretty much the same model utilized by InsWeb, the only difference being that the products offered are loan products, not insurance products. As

■ Changes in brokerage trading value of each company

Shares in the market brokerage trading value in 4Q of fiscal year ended March 2006

(billion yen)

Ranked first among all securities firms

SBI E*TRADE surpassed Nomura Securities in 4Q of fiscal year ended March 2005

SBI E*TRADE SECURITIES: 28,371 (10.68%)

Nomura Securities: 19,279 (7.26%)

Matsui: 10,752 (4.05%)

Daiwa SMBC: 9,440 (3.55%)

Nikko Citigroup: 7,509 (2.83%)

Daiwa: 6,184 (2.33%)

Nikko Cordial: 2,623 (0.99%)

1Q 2Q 3Q 4Q	1Q 2Q 3Q 4Q	1Q 2Q 3Q 4Q	1Q 2Q 3Q 4Q	1Q 2Q 3Q 4Q
Fiscal year ended March 2002	Fiscal year ended March 2003	Fiscal year ended March 2004	Fiscal year ended March 2005	Fiscal year ended March 2006

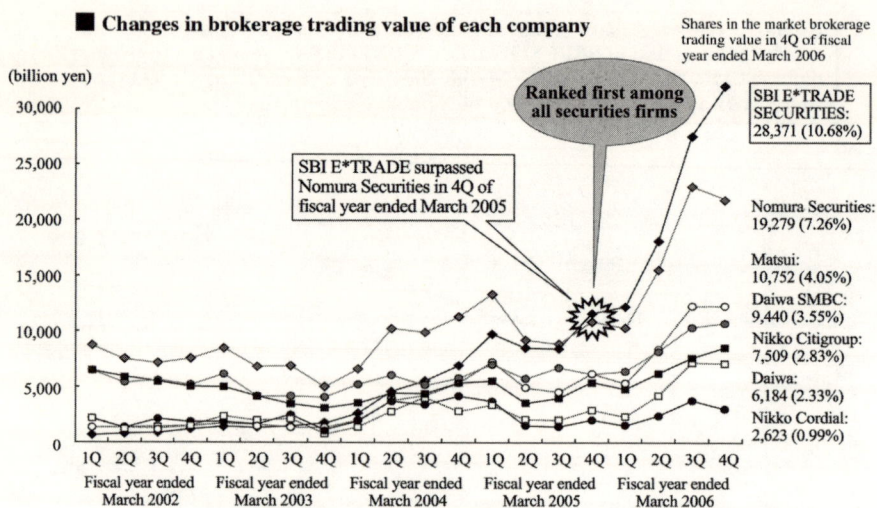

* Figures shown in parentheses represent the share of each company, which is calculated by dividing the company's brokerage trading value, by the market brokerage trading value in the three major markets (i.e., Tokyo, Osaka, and Nagoya Stock Exchanges).

EXHIBIT 2.9 Comparison of SBI E*TRADE SECURITIES with Major Securities Firms in Terms of Brokerage Trading Value

Source: This information was compiled by the SBI Group based on the official figures released by each securities firm and the Tokyo Stock Exchange.

with InsWeb, E-LOAN provides a marketplace wherein a number of financial institutions come together and display a variety of loan products. Consumers who wish to use loans can compare and study the various loan products offered by different financial institutions and apply for those loans that they like. The fact of the matter is that applying for a loan is not always a very pleasant experience. The services that are offered by E-LOAN are intended to help ease the psychological discomfort that normally accompanies this experience, lower the information barrier with an application procedure that is as simple as possible, and allow consumers to make a sensible decision that will sit well with them. This service would not have been possible had it not been for the emergence of the Internet.

Both InsWeb and E-LOAN originally started out as joint ventures with U.S. companies. Eventually, however, we acquired all the shares that were held by their U.S. respective partners and made changes to their business models to suit the Japanese market. Today, each has grown to become the largest in the Japanese marketplace within its own product category, continuing to grow at a steady pace. In 2004 the marketplace business expanded into nonfinancial fields with mover quotes and home renovation quotes, among other things, using this same basic business model.

Housing Loan System and SBI Mortgage. Around 1999, I began to think about how I might create a new housing loan system in Japan. Under the housing loan system existing in Japan in those days, the funding needs of homebuyers were met primarily by housing loans provided in the form of low-interest rate public corporation loans from the Government Housing Loan Corporation, which financed the loans through the Fiscal Investment and Loan Program, or mortgage loans from regular banks, which financed the loans with funds deposited at the bank, or a combination of these two forms. Based on loan balances, housing loans provided through the Government Housing Loan Corporation accounted for about 42 percent of the overall housing loan market. I knew then that this market situation would not last too long, and that it was only a matter of time before significant reforms were implemented. The reason was that, in a sense, Japan's public finance was already cash strapped at that point, and I knew that the Government Housing Loan Corporation's mechanism itself, which relied on the government's Fiscal Investment and Loan Program as its source of funds, simply could not survive much longer. In addition, I was also aware that public corporation loans, which offered a low and long-term fixed interest rate, could not possibly compete in a deregulated interest rate environment. In those days, the interest rates offered by the Government Housing Loan Corporation were set at 0.2 percent to 0.5 percent lower than the rate offered by private-sector financial institutions, and they were even lower than the interest rate earned on funds deposited with the Fiscal Investment and Loan Program, creating a negative interest rate spread. As I had anticipated, this form of housing loan system soon began to break down.

In June 2005, the Law on Japan Housing Finance Agency was enacted. As a result, the Government Housing Loan Corporation, which holds housing loan receivables amounting to nearly 55 trillion yen, is to be abolished effective April 1, 2007, and its operations will be transferred to the Japan Housing Finance Agency, which is an independent administrative agency. In view of the purpose of the reform of special public corporations, that is, "what can be done by the private sector should be left in its hands," it was decided that the said agency would gradually phase out its loan business and review its interest rate schedule. In the future, the primary business of the agency will be to provide support in the purchase and securitization of receivables from housing loans provided by banks, as well as the sale of these receivables in the market after they have been repackaged.

Asset Management and Venture Capital Funds. Let's move on to our last example, the asset management business. In the spring of 2000, I launched a venture capital fund that was filled with features that were considered rather unusual at that time. What was so unusual about the fund was, first of all, its size. The fund raised a massive amount of capital—some 150.5 billion yen—in one shot. Up to that point, the most a venture capital fund could raise at a time was only about 20 to 30 billion yen. The second thing that was rather unusual was that a majority of the money the fund had raised was invested heavily in group companies operating within the Internet field. A typical venture capital fund would allocate the money that it had raised to a variety of business segments.

Third, it was particularly unusual that the fund had an investment period of only 5 years (with an optional 2-year extension), as a typical venture capital fund would normally have an investment period of about 10 years.

Of course, it was I who made the decision to create the fund with these unusual features, but the decision came after much debate within myself. At that time, Japan was several years behind the United States with respect to the Internet industry. Therefore, at the time of the inception of the fund there were practically no venture firms in Japan that would qualify for the 150.5 billion yen that we had raised. I was not sure if enough companies worthy of our money would show up in succession and become successful enough to make an initial public offering within the fund's investment period. So I studied the advancement of the Internet in the United States, how it had developed as an industry, and the speed of such development. At the same time, I became convinced that, in light of Japan's track record of past achievements during the process of catching up with the major Western industrialized nations, if we invested the massive 150.5 billion yen into the Japanese Internet industry, then we would be able to gain a respectable return on our investment even within five years.

The outcome of our investment was very close to what I had expected. Once the fund had entered into the full-scale payback period, we requested the fund's investors to approve a two-year extension with the intention of taking on the challenge of earning a better investment return.

This gigantic flagship fund has basically completed its activity in making new investments, excluding investments in companies that are very likely to go public at a later stage. We have already launched a next-generation flagship fund, the Broadband Fund, in April 2005 with an initial capital of 53.5 billion yen. As a satellite fund of the Broadband Fund, we created a fund with an initial capital of 20.0 billion yen, which that was provided by Fuji Television Network, Inc., Nippon Broadcasting System, Inc., and the SBI Group. The fund invests in venture firms that are engaged primarily in the content business, which provides visual images, music, and publications, among other things, and media- and broadband-related businesses.

Biotechnology, along with the Internet, is likely to become one of the core industries in the twenty-first century. In December 2003 we launched a fund that invests principally in biotechnology venture firms. The size of this fund now exceeds 10.0 billion yen. We have also established corporate restructuring funds (including a mezzanine fund) aimed at rehabilitating companies that went bankrupt following the collapse of the economic bubble, and these funds have thus far produced healthy investment results.

HISTORY OF THE SBI GROUP: FIVE STAGES

The changes taking place in the organization of the SBI Group may be divided into five distinct stages. In this section, I explain each of these five stages in detail.

Stage 1: Creation of Operating Companies

The first thing we did was to create subsidiaries in each business segment and establish various business lines within the group.

As I discuss in Chapter 1, at the time of the group's formation two main events were taking place that would trigger significant structural changes in the financial industry.

The first factor was the Financial Big Bang, which finally brought a wave of deregulation to Japan some 20 years later than its occurrence in the United States, and about 10 years later than its occurrence in the United Kingdom.

The other major event was the Internet Revolution. The popularity of the Internet has brought on a tremendous price-cutting effect, as well as consumer and investor sovereignty. The Internet has also prompted the creation of a new marketplace for comparing and searching various products, in addition to new markets for various goods and services, and so on, and has created a platform for various networks to compete against one another.

In addition, if I were to add another event that triggered structural changes in the financial industry, that would be the collapse of the economic bubble followed by the reorganization of the industry itself.

At the time of the group's formation, all of these events were taking place almost simultaneously. In other words, the process of creative destruction encircling the financial industry was about to unfold, the result of which would be the creation of new types of finance and a new order in the industry.

Amidst such a situation, we decided to take advantage of the enormous destructive power that existed within the Internet in order to offer higher economic value and convenience to investors and consumers. The first thing we did was to create 44 subsidiaries under the umbrella

A number of subsidiaries engaged in financial related businesses were
established in succession under Softbank Finance. Under the direct
control of the parent, the subsidiaries would pursue their businesses while
maximizing the synergetic effects generated within themselves.

Peak number of operating subsidiaries: 44

EXHIBIT 2.10 Stage 1: Creation of Operating Companies

of Softbank Finance (see Exhibit 2.10). We created these subsidiaries in
succession in order to determine which companies were compatible
with the Internet community or compatible with the existing markets.

Stage 2: Positioning of Core Companies

In the next stage, we created what is referred to as our "core companies," namely, E*Trade Securities Co., Ltd., Softbank Investment Corporation, Morningstar Japan K.K., and Finance All Corporation. In an
attempt to reorganize the 44 subsidiaries that existed at that point, we
consolidated various companies using similar business models under
each of these core companies.

We then created a structure wherein certain functions that had
been previously assumed by Softbank Finance could now be taken

> **Those group companies that had similar business lines and models were consolidated under each core company in the same field. Certain functions assumed by Softbank Finance were now taken over by Softbank Investment, E*Trade Securities, and other core companies.**

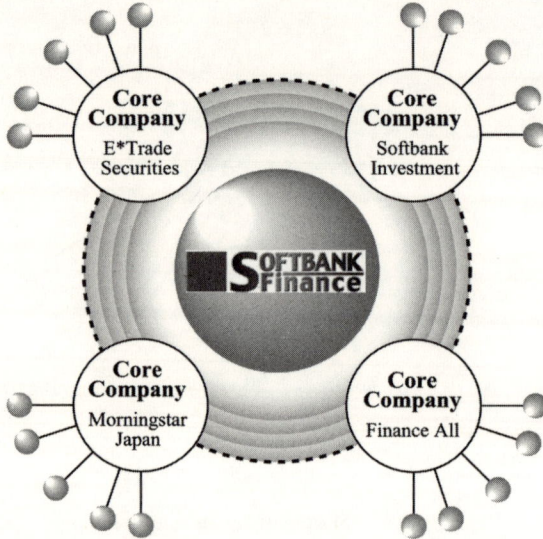

EXHIBIT 2.11   Stage 2: Positioning of the Core Companies

over by Softbank Investment, E*Trade Securities, Morningstar Japan, and Finance All as the core companies (see Exhibit 2.11).

At this point, the SBI Group, which had established operating companies in every field of the financial industry, excluding banking, and had steadily developed the business basis of the group, reached a level where significant synergies were created between the group companies.

However, we all know that if you continue to blow air into a balloon, it will eventually burst. By the same token, I thought that if we continued to expand the size of the group, we would be at increased risk of facing the following situations:

- It would be increasingly difficult to maintain an orderly ecosystem heading in one direction.

As I mentioned earlier, our group is moving in one direction, or shall I say, following a vector. That vector signifies that we were moving toward a near-future vision of the financial industry that we consider ideal. However, it concerned me that this sense of direction might fall apart should the group continue to expand, perhaps even with nonfinancial businesses becoming involved.

- Even the slightest distortion at a distance from the core of the Group's ecosystem could lead to a meltdown of the overall ecosystem.

I feared that this could happen in the future.

We must detect in advance any problems that might take place in the future and undertake efforts to prevent them from actually occurring. I therefore decided to implement the following strategies before any problems were allowed to surface.

Strategic Reorganization and Integration. First, through a "strategic reorganization and integration" within the group, I decided to create a mechanism for forming multiple core companies and fostering their self-growth. I also thought it was necessary to introduce a system that could enable the effective sharing of customer bases within the group ecosystem.

This strategy is based on the concept that self-organization through the formation of core companies (another concept proposed by complexity science) will naturally generate an overall order. In other words, such self-organization should be promoted to create order in an advanced form.

To put it differently, by forming multiple core companies within a group and placing under each core company subsidiaries with common customer targets, the core company and its subsidiaries could work together to effectively realize a further expansion of their customer base and to broaden an ecosystem that centers on the core company, which will in turn increase its ability in self-growth.

As it was no longer possible for me to look after every business of our group at this point, I needed to create core companies and allow each of them to handle the companies under its umbrella, sharing the same business model or customer base.

There are four requirements which each core company must fulfill.

1. The company has already made a public offering of its shares, or is expected to do so in the near future.
2. The company is capable of raising funds on its own through a public offering and possesses enough financial muscle to form a group of companies under its umbrella.
3. The company is currently maintaining, or may maintain in the near future, a predominantly leading position in the business territory in which it operates.
4. The company must steadily increase its free cash flow on a consolidated basis and maximize its shareholder value based on this consolidated free cash flow.

From the Birth of a Small Ecosystem to a Large Ecosystem. The plan here was to start with a small ecosystem that centered on core companies that met these requirements and allowed all the members comprising the ecosystem to cooperate with one another in order to effectively expand their shared customer base.

I would then put together several small ecosystems to form a large ecosystem that would continuously evolve as a group, driven as a large vector.

For example, I put together Morningstar Asset Management Co., Ltd., E*Advisor Co., Ltd., and Gomez Consulting Co., Ltd. under Morningstar Japan. Gomez Consulting, which has grown quite rapidly in recent years, primarily carries out comparative research and the ranking of various e-commerce web sites. For example, the company would find out which online securities are superior to others by comparing various online securities firms and ranking them based on scores that reflected their overall evaluation.

Under Finance All, I put together a variety of businesses, such as InsWeb, E-LOAN, Good Mortgage Corporation (currently SBI Mortgage Co., Ltd.), Web-Lease Co., Ltd. (currently SBI Lease Co., Ltd.), Finance

All Service (currently SBI Financial Agency Co., Ltd.), and E-LOAN Direct, which subsequently changed its corporate name to SBI Mortgage Consulting Co., Ltd., which in turn was merged into SBI Mortgage Co., Ltd.). The businesses of these companies largely fall into either one of two distinct categories: the financial marketplace business or the financial products business.

The financial marketplace business offers consumers financial or insurance product comparisons on a single list. The former InsWeb Japan K.K. and the former E-LOAN Japan Co., Ltd. were absorbed into the Finance All Corporation (the Finance All Corporation now merged into SBI Holdings, Inc.) as the InsWeb Division and the E-LOAN Division, respectively.

The financial products business employs the latest financial technologies to offer consumers unique financial products. The companies that comprise this business include SBI Mortgage Co., Ltd. (formerly Good Mortgage Corporation) and SBI Lease Co., Ltd. (formerly Web-Lease). These companies were put together and allowed to cooperate with one another in order to effectively pursue their businesses.

Stage 3: Careful Selection of the Business Portfolio

At this stage, we reorganized the group companies once again from the perspective of a "selection and concentration" approach in order to clearly determine the core businesses of the group. We would carefully select and build a solid business portfolio that, in addition to existing ideas and concepts, could withstand competition in light of the concept of a core business. To "carefully select" means to pick out those businesses that are not considered core, are unprofitable, or have no future growth potential. So far, we have liquidated only one company, E-Bond Securities Co., Ltd., and have sold four other companies. The remaining companies were either merged with others or moved under different core companies (see Exhibit 2.12).

For example, TechTank Corporation (currently SBI Technology Co., Ltd.) and VeriTrans, Inc. (currently SBI VeriTrans Co., Ltd.), both of

> The core business of the group were clarified. Through a "selection and concentration" approach (i.e., consolidation, liquidation, etc. of group companies), only quality group companies were consolidated under each core company. A carefully selected business portfolio was formed for each core business.

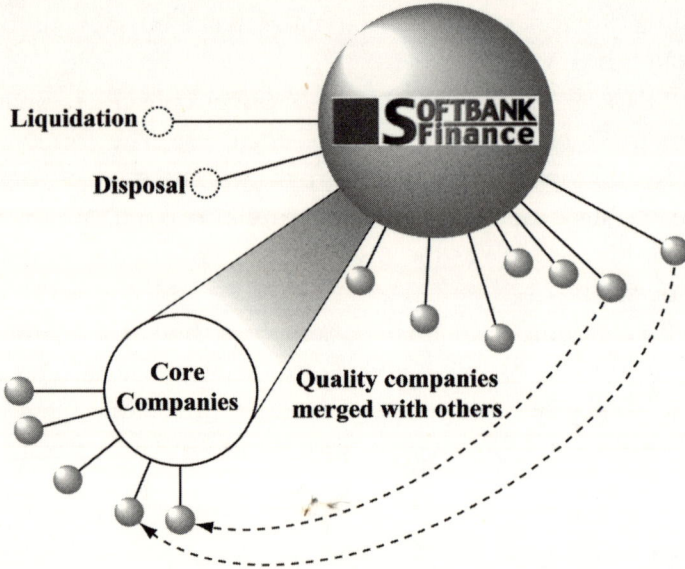

EXHIBIT 2.12   Stage 3: Careful Selection of Business Portfolio

which had been directly owned subsidiaries of Softbank Finance, were moved under the umbrella of Finance All.

TechTank had been originally established as an integration of the systems divisions of the Softbank Finance Group. The realignment of TechTank under the umbrella of Finance All, which operates the Ins-Web Division and the E-LOAN Division, both of which specialize in offering one-list comparison services, made it possible for the company to directly support these businesses and maximize the synergies between various businesses.

SBI VeriTrans provides an electronic payment settlement service for e-commerce businesses. The company has grown significantly in tandem with the increasing popularity of e-commerce. As a company that provides an Internet-related financial service, the company is able to help increase the consolidated earnings of the Finance All Group.

Stage 4: Maximization of the Shareholder Value of an Operating Holding Company

This stage is devoted to the "maximization of the shareholder value of an operating holding company." Softbank Investment Corporation (currently SBI Holdings, Inc.) now began to position itself as an operating holding company, while maintaining the characteristics of a corporate group that was pillared by three core businesses: asset management, brokerage and investment banking, and financial services (see Exhibit 2.13).

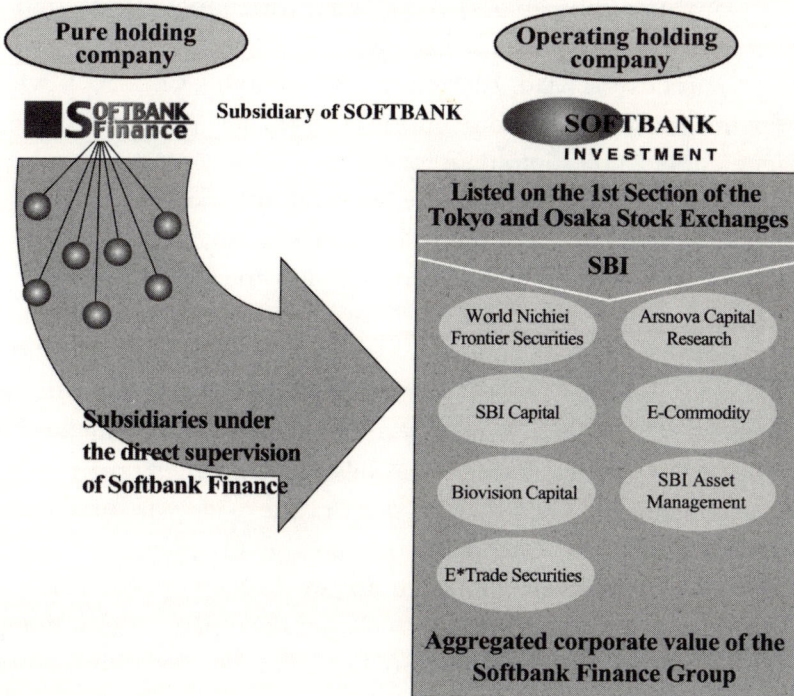

EXHIBIT 2.13   Corporate Value Integration within the Softbank Finance Group Companies

The fact that Softbank Investment, an operating company, was merged with E*Trade Japan K.K., a holding company with E*Trade Securities under its umbrella, suggests that the new Softbank Investment now possessed the characteristics of both an operating company and a holding company. In other words, we made the decision that Softbank Investment would exist as an operating holding company for some time to come. The core businesses of the new Softbank Investment would be asset management, brokerage and investment banking, and financial services.

It may even be said that the merger made it such that the operating holding company would be able to explore various business opportunities in the future, while maintaining these three core businesses.

The merger itself was meant to reorganize the companies within the group, but it was designed so that the postmerger operating holding company would be able to assimilate a wide range of external resources into the group. A case in point is the acquisition of World Nichiei Securities Co., Ltd. (currently SBI Securities Co., Ltd.), which was an important part of our effort to assimilate powerful external management resources into the group.

The same thing was true of the acquisition of Nissho Iwai Securities Co., Ltd., which subsequently changed its corporate name to Fides Securities Corporation, which in turn was absorbed by E*Trade Securities. The purpose of these acquisitions was to further strengthen the three core businesses through the assimilation of influential external management resources into the group (see Exhibit 2.14).

Because Softbank Investment is an operating holding company, we basically took steps to guide the promising companies under its umbrella into making IPOs in succession in line with our fundamental business development concepts as described in Chapter 1. E*Trade Securities went public. So did Finance All. World Nichiei Securities (currently SBI Securities) became a publicly held company after it merged with an already-public company, Softbank Frontier Securities. As part of the strategy to consolidate all publicly held group companies under the umbrella of Softbank Investment, the 37.72 percent interest in Finance All that had been held by Softbank Finance was entirely trans-

SBI now began to position itself as an operation holding company, while maintaining the characteristics of a corporate group pillared by three core businesses.

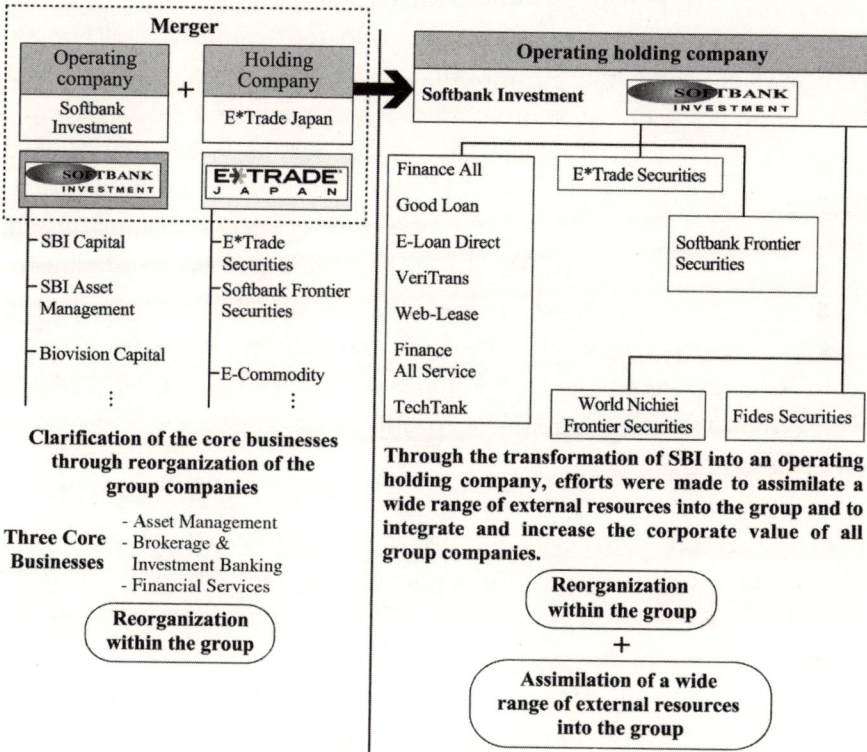

Merger

Operating company — Softbank Investment

+

Holding Company — E*Trade Japan

→

Operating holding company

Softbank Investment

- SBI Capital
- SBI Asset Management
- Biovision Capital
⋮

- E*Trade Securities
- Softbank Frontier Securities
- E-Commodity
⋮

Finance All
Good Loan
E-Loan Direct
VeriTrans
Web-Lease
Finance All Service
TechTank

E*Trade Securities

Softbank Frontier Securities

World Nichiei Frontier Securities

Fides Securities

Clarification of the core businesses through reorganization of the group companies

Three Core Businesses
- Asset Management
- Brokerage & Investment Banking
- Financial Services

Reorganization within the group

Through the transformation of SBI into an operating holding company, efforts were made to assimilate a wide range of external resources into the group and to integrate and increase the corporate value of all group companies.

Reorganization within the group

+

Assimilation of a wide range of external resources into the group

EXHIBIT 2.14 Stage 4: Maximization of Shareholder Value of an Operating Holding Company

ferred to Softbank Investment. In addition, Finance All increased its capital through the issuance of new shares by way of third-party allotment to Softbank Investment, and through this transaction Softbank Investment owned 44.90 percent of the shares in Finance All. As a result, the business results of Finance All were now incorporated into the consolidated results of Softbank Investment.

Up to this point, Softbank Finance had been the parent company of Finance All. Softbank Finance is a wholly owned subsidiary of SOFTBANK CORP., and its business results were fully reflected in the consolidated results of SOFTBANK CORP. This fact alone is not a problem in the least. However, things reached the point where Finance All had practically no impact on the consolidated results of SOFTBANK CORP. Whether Finance All reported a 500 million yen increase or a 300 million yen increase in ordinary profit, made virtually no difference to the overall results of SOFTBANK CORP. Similarly, Finance All had no impact on the share price or shareholder value of SOFTBANK CORP. However, it was quite a different story when the business results of Finance All were reflected in the consolidated results of Softbank Investment. As demonstrated by this case, my intention was to continuously improve the consolidated business results of Softbank Investment, which was now an operating holding company, by having the results of its group companies manifest a pronounced impact on the overall group results.

To review, through the merger with E*Trade Japan, Softbank Investment transformed itself into an operating holding company. The point here is that in order to maximize the shareholder value of Softbank Investment as an operating holding company, not only does it need to rely on its internal resources, but it also must actively assimilate a wide range of external resources into its group of companies. In other words, the intention is to realize a dramatic increase in the shareholder value of Softbank Investment by consolidating the different shareholder value of the various companies within the Softbank Finance Group and assimilating various external resources into Softbank Investment.

Keep in mind that Softbank Investment is listed on the first section of the Tokyo Stock Exchange and is at times ranked top ten in terms of trading value. Its shares are highly liquid, and the company is fully capable of raising funds in the capital market. As a result, the company possesses very advantageous elements for realizing various proposed acquisitions. My fundamental idea was to aggressively assimilate useful external resources into Softbank Investment in order to help increase its shareholder value.

Before the transition to a holding company system

Softbank Investment Corporation

> Venture fund management business

July 1, 2005 Corporation name change →

After the transition to a holding company system

SBI Holdings, Inc.

Transfer of the venture fund management business

BIOVISION Capital Corp.

Fund management business | Asset Management: Softbank Investment Corp. (Formerly SBI Ventures K.K.)

Softbank Contents Partners Corporation

Merger of three companies

Brokerage & Investment Banking

Financial Services

SBI Ventures Corporation

Non-financial fields

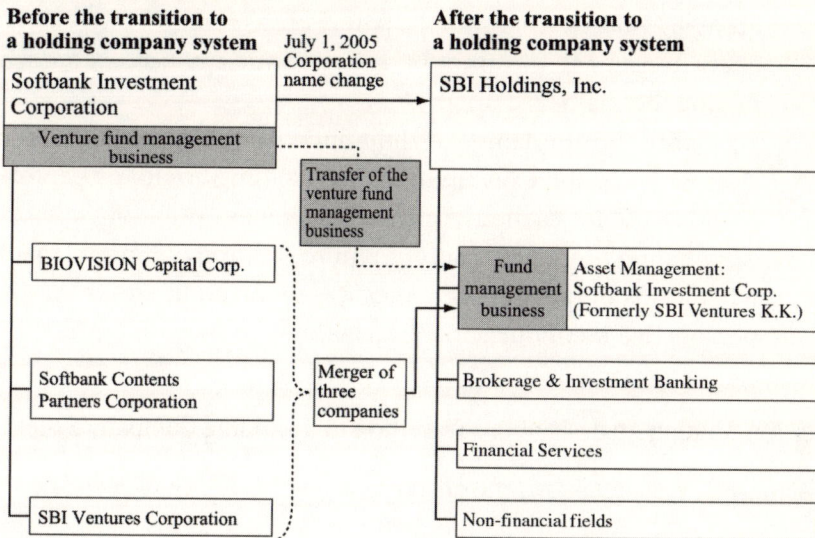

EXHIBIT 2.15 Stage 5: Transition to a Holding Company System

Stage 5: Transition to a Holding Company System

On July 1, 2005, Softbank Investment Corporation changed its corporation name to SBI Holdings, Inc., and as a result, the SBI Group made a transition to a holding company system (see Exhibit 2.15). Before making the decision to proceed with this move, I pondered three points, in much the same way as I had debated seven years back when first forming the group.

1. Whether the SBI Group had produced results as expected over the six-year period during which the group had formed as a type of business ecosystem, and whether each company comprising this ecosystem had produced better results than those that would have been produced if the company had been operating on a standalone basis. Stated another way, the question is whether the group had created a status that was consistent with the main propositions of the complexity of knowledge: "A mass, which is composed of multiple parts, must be larger than

an aggregate of the multiple parts" and "a mass contains new characteristics that cannot be found in the multiple parts comprising the mass."

2. To clarify the fundamental difference between a pure holding company and the existing operating holding company centered on Softbank Investment from a management point of view.

3. Concerning the ideal vision of a pure holding company, that is, what kinds of business activities it is involved in and from what perspective it conducts these activities.

Decision-Making Analysis of the Transition to a Holding Company System

The analysis was based on the aforementioned three questions.

1. *Did the SBI Group produce results as expected?* As far as this question is concerned, the answer is yes if we look objectively at the business results of the group up to this point. That is to say that the organizational strategies we have implemented up to this point may be considered largely appropriate. In particular, I believe that our consistent strategy of forming a group centered on Softbank Investment over the years has proved to be very effective. As a venture capital firm, Softbank Investment had invested in a number of Internet-related venture firms and had provided support, not only financial but also managerial support from all aspects, until they went public. Therefore, the knowledge, know-how, and experience that Softbank Investment had acquired from this primary business also helped the SBI Group to foster our own group companies. A number of companies have attempted to create new businesses through undertaking internal ventures, intragroup ventures, and so on, but it appears that they have not had much success so far. I believe that our strategy as such has been one of the major factors contributing to nine of our group companies going public within a short period of time, spanning only several years.

2. *What is the difference between an operating holding company and a pure holding company?* The second point that I pondered was the difference between an operating holding company and a pure holding company. I examine this point in general terms.

In Japan, the restrictions on pure holding companies were lifted completely in December 1997. In March 1998, the restrictions on financial holding companies were also removed. The pure holding company structure has not been around very long. Although there are no longer restrictions, this organizational form has not been widely put into practice. The operating holding company has always been the more commonly used organizational form over the pure holding company form. Similarly, the pure holding company form has long been recognized in the United States, but has never gained much popularity. We normally find that this organizational form is used only by financial institutions or public utility enterprises, which are subject to restrictions on the conduct of their business activities in more than one state. In Europe, however, the pure holding company structure has been adopted by a large number of companies. Hence, it would appear that a transition to the pure holding company structure might not turn out to be an absolute must. However, it does appear to have the following distinct benefits.

First of all, unlike a pure holding company, in the case of an operating holding company there is a chance that the operational decision making in the operating groups of the parent company may be confused with the strategic decision making for the overall group. Unless the CEO constantly takes the approach of making decisions for the overall group even when he or she attends meetings of the board of directors, only the parent company's businesses tend to be discussed at these meetings. Therefore, strategic decisions for the overall group may not be adequately discussed or may even be ignored from time to time.

In a pure holding company, on the other hand, the capacity for building medium- to long-term management strategies is completely separated from the business operations capacity. Therefore, financial self-sufficiency is clearly established for each business unit, and strategic freedom in business operations can be ensured to a fairly large extent.

In addition, as is often pointed out, in the case of an operating holding company it is easy to create a contrastive approach based on a parent-versus-subsidiaries mentality, and the notion that the parent must manage its subsidiaries often penetrates deeply within the group. It is often considered a negative aspect when a parent sends its employees to work at subsidiaries on a long-term assignment, or a parent permanently transfers its employees to subsidiaries. Sometimes, subsidiaries may become overly dependent upon the parent.

In the case of a pure holding company, a horizontal bond is often created among the group companies engaged in business activities, and, as such, there is no internal hierarchy within the group. As a result, human resources within the group become more mobile, and it is easy to strategically assign appropriate employees to appropriate positions. In addition, it is easy to implement a groupwide, merit-based personnel evaluation system and to nurture human capital across the group, including the top management executives who will play a major role in the future.

Furthermore, further penetration of the said horizontal bond enables the employees of various group companies to communicate with one another more often and to increase the group management resources to be shared within the group.

3. *What is the "ideal form" of a pure holding company?* Now we cover the ideal form and functions of a pure holding company. Since a pure holding company is a "long-term largest shareholder" from the point of view of its subsidiaries and affiliated companies, its primary responsibility should be to act as a corporate governance entity. To put it more specifically, in much the same way as the corporate value of its subsidiaries and af-

filiated companies continuously increases, a pure holding company, as their largest shareholder, should thoroughly monitor the group and take necessary actions on a timely basis. It needs to fulfill the following specific functions:

- Establishment and dissemination of a group management philosophy.
- Establishment and dissemination of a group vision.
- Establishment and promotion of a group growth strategy.
- Building and management of a group business portfolio based on the growth strategy of the group (including the revision of the business portfolio and the reorganization of the group).
- Effective allocation of group management resources based on the growth strategy of the group.
- Creation and management of group management resources (including the brands, know-how, technologies, and so on owned by the group as a whole).
- Groupwide human capital and training, corporate communications (CC) activities such as IR and PR, and corporate social responsibility (CSR) activities as well as fund-raising, legal affairs, and other activities that need to be undertaken as a group.
- Maintenance of the cohesive power of the group.

I examined the three points previously outlined from an organizational and theoretical point of view and gave much consideration to the current trends in government administration, as well as the future growth strategy of the SBI Group. Ultimately, I decided to make a transition to a pure holding company system (to be precise, we are not a pure holding company at the moment because the real estate business unit still exists within the group as part of our transitional measures). This transition has three immediate goals, as follows:

1. We will establish an integrated financial group that is at the forefront of the current trend toward conglomeration within the financial industry.

Our transition to a pure holding company system is also consistent with the Japanese government's view in favor of the promotion of the conglomeration of financial institutions that transcends existing boundaries that are based on business types within the financial industry.

2. We will build a business portfolio that allows us to exhaustively pursue synergies between the group companies. On the basis of the SBI Group's management philosophy and vision, we will seek to enhance the efficiency in our business portfolio by strategically adding and reshuffling components of the portfolio.

3. We will establish an organizational structure that will allow us to "expand beyond the financial field by leveraging our core financial businesses."

No longer under the scope of consolidation of SOFTBANK CORP. and no longer subjected to the various restrictions on our business domains, we will seek to realize a smooth entry into nonfinancial fields at an accelerated pace.

I conceive that the transition to a pure holding company system will enable us to enhance the unified power of the SBI Group as a business ecosystem and to increase the corporate value of the group at an accelerated pace (see Exhibit 2.16).

Before this section ends, I would like to mention for reference, four types of domestic financial conglomerates according to the definitions given in the guidelines for the supervision of financial conglomerates released by the Financial Services Agency, which is about to officially start considering the introduction of a "law concerning financial conglomerates."

According to the guidelines, there are four types of financial conglomerates: (1) Financial holding company group: a group in which a financial institution controls, under its umbrella, a bank, an insurance company, a securities firm, and the like; (2) de facto holding company group: a group in which a general (nonfinancial) firm controls, under

Growth Stages of Business Ecosystem

Establishment/ Expansion

Market Domination

Self- Growth

Flow of organization building

Stage 1 Create subsidiaries in each business segment and establish various business lines within the group.

Stage 2 Consolidate synergy-maximizing group companies under the core companies to enhance the business development capacity of the group.

Stage 3 Clarify the "core businesses" of the group and reorganize the group companies once again from the perspective of a "selection and concentration" approach and build a business portfolio that is selected carefully for each core business.

Stage 4 1. Consolidate once again the main group companies under an operating holding company to maximize the corporate value of the operating holding company.

2. Fully take advantage of the business bases and fundraising capacity of the operating holding company, and assimilate external management resources through acquisitions and mergers in order to further strengthen each core business.

Stage 5 1. Transition to a pure holding company.

2. The pure holding company is listed on the first section of the Tokyo Stock Exchange.

3. Enhance the overall power of the SBI Group as a corporate ecosystem in order to increase its corporate value at an accelerated pace.

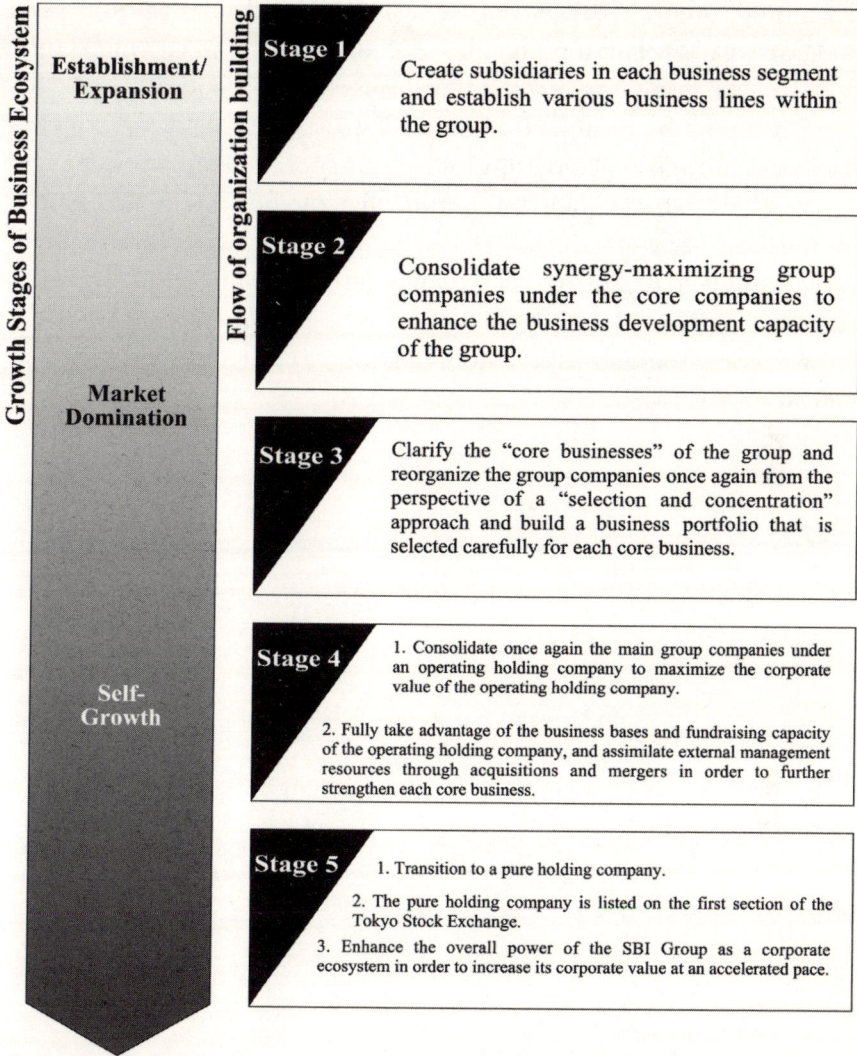

EXHIBIT 2.16   Flow of Organization Building Within the SBI Group

its umbrella, more than two of the following financial institutions: a bank, an insurance company, and a securities firm; (3) financial institution parent company group: a group in which the parent, which is either a bank, an insurance company, or a securities firm, controls, under its umbrella, subsidiaries that are financial subsidiaries engaged in types of business that differ from that of the parent; (4) foreign holding company group, and so on: a group in which a foreign financial holding company or the like controls its branches and subsidiaries in Japan.

According to this classification, the SBI Group is deemed to fall under category (2).

CHAPTER 3

Vision of the New SBI Group

CRITERIA FOR CREATING THE SBI GROUP'S VISION

In creating the SBI Group's vision, I felt that such vision must fulfill certain criteria such as those described next.

First, the vision must be clearly defined.

Second, it must align all group company employees with the strategic direction of the businesses of the group, and raise the level of motivation in their work.

Third, it must have a high likelihood of being realized.

Finally, it must bring desirable benefits and value to all stakeholders.

With these four criteria in mind, we established the following three objectives as the vision of the new SBI Group (see Exhibit 3.1):

1. We will work to maximize our corporate value with a firm foundation based on customer value, enhancing the synergies between shareholder and human capital values.
2. We aim to increase the aggregate market capitalization of the listed companies within the group (including subsidiaries and affiliated companies consolidated under the equity method)

from the current 1.0 trillion yen to 3.0 trillion yen in three years and 5.0 trillion yen in five years.

3. We aim to become not just a "strong company," but a "strong and respected company."

Now permit me to elaborate a little further upon each of the three objectives.

Maximize Corporate Value

The first part of our group vision is to maximize our corporate value with a firm foundation based on customer value, enhancing the synergies between shareholder and human capital values. I have already explained in Chapter 1 what kinds of value are shared within the SBI Group. Our fundamental understanding is that corporate value is an aggregate of customer value, shareholder value, and human capital

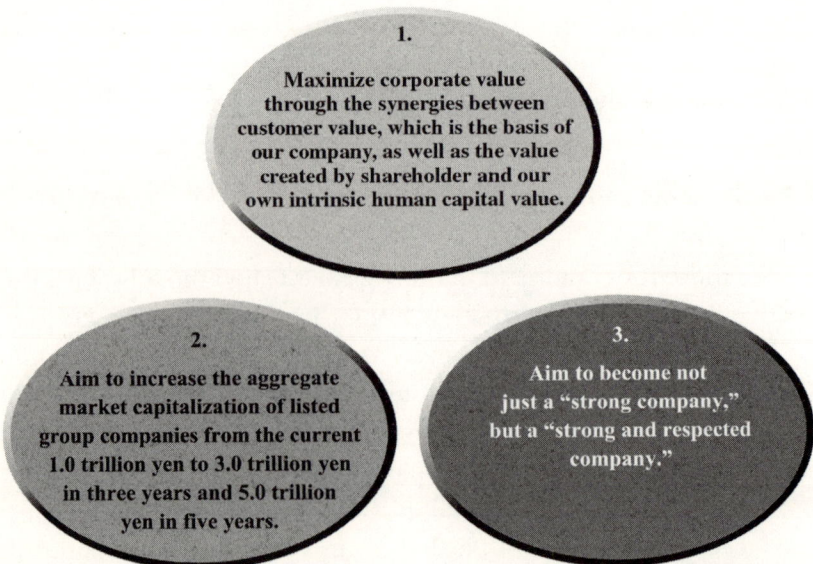

1.
Maximize corporate value through the synergies between customer value, which is the basis of our company, as well as the value created by shareholder and our own intrinsic human capital value.

2.
Aim to increase the aggregate market capitalization of listed group companies from the current 1.0 trillion yen to 3.0 trillion yen in three years and 5.0 trillion yen in five years.

3.
Aim to become not just a "strong company," but a "strong and respected company."

EXHIBIT 3.1   Vision of the New SBI Group (1)

value. I also state that, with the creation of customer value as a foundation, corporate value is generated and increased through mutual linkages with shareholder value and human capital value.

As far as our understanding is concerned, customer value forms a foundation and is our first principle. Customer value is created through the offering of goods and services that customers find useful. We are able to increase our customer value by continually increasing customer satisfaction through improving the quality of the goods and services that we offer and lowering their prices. In this sense, I have continually stressed the importance of adhering to a customer-centric principle throughout all of our businesses within the organization, if we wish to continue to grow as a group. My intention is to continue to hold onto this view as the basis of our vision for the new SBI Group.

Increase Aggregate Market Capitalization to 3.0 Trillion Yen in Three Years and 5.0 Trillion Yen in Five Years

The second part of the group vision is to increase the aggregate market capitalization of the listed companies within the group (including subsidiaries and affiliated companies consolidated under the equity method) from the current 1.0 trillion yen to 3.0 trillion yen in three years and 5.0 trillion yen in five years. This aspect is fairly straightforward as it sets forth specific target figures (see Exhibit 3.2).

With the goal of forming an Internet-based financial group, the SBI Group initiated operations in April 1999 by establishing Softbank Finance Corporation with 55 members from SOFTBANK's former Administration Group, which was under my authority. Using Softbank Finance as the parent company, we created the SBI Group as a business ecosystem. As of November 2005, nine of our group companies are listed companies, and their aggregate market capitalization has grown to nearly 1 trillion yen.

It has taken us almost six years to reach this point, and words cannot describe the hardships that we have endured and the tremendous effort that we have applied to create the businesses and customer base

**Group aggregate market capitalization target:
3 trillion yen in three years and 5 trillion yen in five years**

> Aiming to increase the aggregate market capitalization of the listed companies within the group from the current 1.0 trillion yen to 3.0 trillion yen in three years and 5.0 trillion yen in five years.

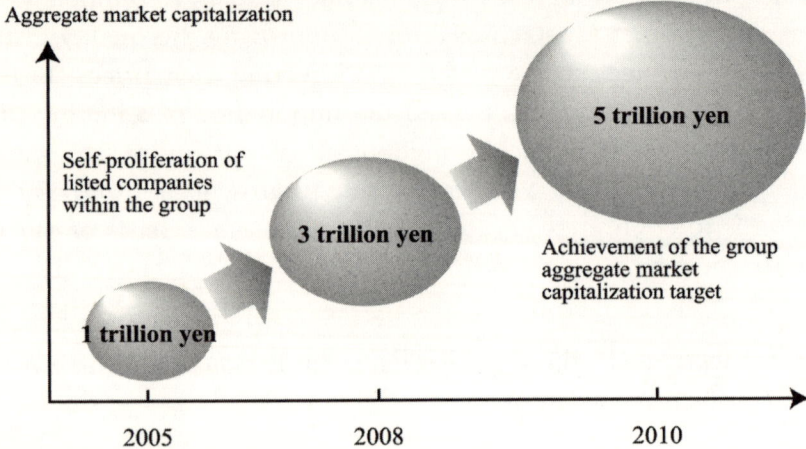

Aggregate market capitalization

Self-proliferation of
listed companies
within the group

5 trillion yen

3 trillion yen

Achievement of the group
aggregate market
capitalization target

1 trillion yen

2005   2008   2010

EXHIBIT 3.2   Vision of the New SBI Group (2)

from scratch. Yet today, I feel that all the hard work has paid off, and looking back I can even say it was quite a joy. I also believe this feeling is timelessly shared today by my colleagues.

In view of the tremendous efforts that we made when first starting the group, I'm quite certain that the chances are decent that we will be able to increase the aggregate market capitalization of listed companies within the group to 3.0 trillion yen over the next three years and even to 5.0 trillion yen within five years; it actually reached 2.6406 trillion yen on January 16, 2006. It goes without saying that we must plan and implement an effective group business strategy to realize this group vision.

Four Strategies to Achieve the Target

Four concrete strategies to achieve the target figures set forth in this group vision are:

1. To make each of the listed group companies self-grow and self-proliferate (see Exhibit 3.3). This is discussed in Chapter 4.
2. To guide the unlisted companies within the group toward a public offering (IPO). There are a number of promising companies within our group that are yet to be listed, and I intend to continue to establish similar such companies in the future and help them grow to the level at which they are able to take themselves public.

   While guiding group companies toward an IPO is important to increase the shareholder value of the overall group, it should also be given consideration in terms of the cohesive power of the group. While a group company becomes an independent and publicly held company through an IPO, it must also maintain a sense of solidarity as a member of our group and examine in detail unique ways to maintain its cohesion with the group. However, we must obviously plan and implement this under the assumption that this now publicly held company recognizes and finds value in various brands carried by the group, the group's corporate culture, the synergies created between the company and other group companies, and the variety of tangible and intangible assets shared within the group. Otherwise, how could this company have any sense of solidarity or cohesion with the group?
3. The third strategy, although it may sound like a contradiction to what I have just discussed, is to exchange the shares of the already listed group companies for shares of SBI Holdings to make them, once again, wholly owned subsidiaries of SBI Holdings. Through the use of this technique, we will be able to increase the total market capitalization of SBI Holdings, which

Self-Growth and Self-Proliferation of Listed Group Companies

■ Market capitalization of the listed group companies

	Market capitalization at initial listing (based on public offering market value)	Market capitalization as of March 31, 2006	Peak market capitalization
SBI Holdings, Inc. 1st Section of the TSE (8473) (Listed on the former NASDAQ Japan on Dec. 15, 2000) Merged with E*Trade Japan K.K. on Jan. 3, 2003	**159.1 billion yen** (When listed on the former NASDAQ Japan) **50.6 billion yen** (As of the merger)	**846.5 billion yen**	**858.1 billion yen** (Apr. 6, 2006)
SBI E*TRADE SECURITIES Co., Ltd. JASDAQ (8701) Listed on Nov. 30, 2004	**123.7 billion yen**	**851.6 billion yen**	**1,260.0 billion yen** (Jan. 16, 2006)
Finance All Corporation Hercules market of the OSE (8437) Listed on Sept. 19, 2003 (Merged into SBI Holdings, Inc. on Mar. 1, 2006)	**5.4 billion yen**	—	**172.3 billion yen** (Jan. 16, 2006)
SBI Securities Co., Ltd. Hercules market of the OSE (8696) Listed on Aug. 10, 2001 (Created through a merger between World Nichiei Securities and Softbank Frontier Securities on Feb. 2, 2004) (Became a wholly owned subsidiary of SBI Holdings, Inc. on Mar. 1, 2006)	**6.8 billion yen** (Aug. 10, 2001) **135.2 billion yen** (As of the merger)	—	**135.2 billion yen** (Feb. 2, 2004)
SBI Partners Co., Ltd. JASDAQ (9653) (Formerly Bunkahoso Brain Co., Ltd.) Listed on Nov. 20, 1991 (Merged into SBI Holdings, Inc. on Mar. 1, 2006)	**39.4 billion yen**	—	**116.5 billion yen** (Jan. 16, 2006)
Morningstar Japan K.K. Hercules market of the OSE (4765) Listed on Jun. 23, 2000	**101.0 billion yen**	**30.4 billion yen**	**122.7 billion yen** (Jun. 23, 2000)
SBI VeriTrans Co., Ltd. Hercules market of the OSE (3749) Listed on Oct. 5, 2004	**8.3 billion yen**	**24.3 billion yen**	**33.8 billion yen** (Feb. 2, 2006)
Zephyr Co., Ltd. 1st section of the TSE (8882) Listed on July 19, 2000	**9.4 billion yen**	**96.6 billion yen**	**135.8 billion yen** (Dec. 26, 2006)

EXHIBIT 3.3   Strategy to Increase Market Capitalization (1)
Source: QUICK.

will in turn increase the aggregate shareholder value of the overall SBI Group. In the United States, this technique is referred to as "privatization" or "re-privatization," and it has been implemented by a number of corporations.

Recently in Japan as well, there have been signs of a trend toward going private among large corporations (World Co., Ltd. and Pokka Corporation, for example).

For the companies that have gone public but have never raised funds in the capital market for the past 10 years or more, it may be worth at least examining the need and/or costs involved to keep themselves publicly held. Finding out why publicly listed companies have privatized themselves would certainly make an interesting research topic (as a matter of fact, I have done research on a few cases in the United States), but that is beyond the scope of this book. The reason why I have steered the now-listed group companies into an IPO one after another as soon as they met the prescribed listing requirements was to sell a portion of their shares so that we could secure sufficient funds to support the further growth of the group. Without such "profits from public offerings" by the listed group companies, we would not have been able to create the SBI Group as we know it today. As long as we remained under the umbrella of SOFTBANK CORP., this was the only way for us to secure a large amount of funds. I may even say that in the past several years, in an attempt to realize a further expansion of the group from a long-term point of view, I guided some of the now listed companies, which we had established and developed over the years, into an IPO without fully examining (while thinking it was necessary) whether it was truly necessary.

At present, however, the SBI Group is no longer under the control of SOFTBANK CORP. and we have much more freedom to raise funds, so there is no longer a reason to aggressively take our subsidiaries public as we had done in the past.

Going forward, before making a decision to take any group company public, I will certainly give careful consideration to the point of whether such a move will be beneficial for SBI Holdings. In addition, we should probably wait to allow any of our group companies to realize an IPO until the company grows to the position where there is enough value to be gained from publicly offering its shares.

In principle, I believe that any company wishing to be publicly held must satisfy the following criteria:

- It is necessary for the company to improve its IT infrastructure and other large-scale capital investments on an ongoing basis, or to increase its capital due to a business that requires a large amount of working capital, or as a result of business expansion. SBI E*TRADE SECURITIES falls into this category.

- The company is required to maintain a neutral position in the business that it conducts. Examples of companies that fall under this category are Morningstar Japan, which rates investment trusts, and Gomez Consulting, which evaluates and ranks companies in various industry categories.

- The company creates little synergies between itself and other group companies, and from the perspective of the group's overall business portfolio, it would be beneficial for the company to publicly offer its shares so that its shareholder value could be actualized, or if the company's significance in the overall group strategy has deteriorated.

If any group company falls under these categories, then we will certainly consider a public offering of its shares. I will consider making it a rule not to allow a public offering by any group company that does not meet these criteria, and I intend to carefully review all group companies that have already begun preparations for an IPO.

In addition, we could even privatize those companies that have already gone public but do not satisfy these criteria in order to increase the shareholder value of SBI Holdings.

Such a move could be, depending upon the market capitalization of each already listed group company, a tool for increasing the value of the overall group.

Of course, the decision to privatize these companies would be based on the premise that, by making them wholly owned subsidiaries and thus increasing our flexibility in implementing a group strategy, we would be able to effectively pursue the synergies between various group companies and incorporate the external and internal management resources of other groups into our organization to make it easy for us to further expand our businesses.

The subtitle of this book is *Continuously Evolving Management*. I decided to give the book this title because I felt that we would need a new strategy for every new stage that we embark upon. We have transformed ourselves through several stages, from a subsidiary of SOFTBANK CORP. to an affiliated company of the corporation consolidated under the equity method, and to the establishment of SBI Holdings and the transition to a pure holding company with the goal of further expanding the distribution of our business ecosystem (i.e., expansion beyond the financial field by leveraging our core financial businesses). Under the circumstances, in some cases, I have had no choice but to mercilessly crush the expectations and dreams of fellow workers who have worked hard toward the realization of an IPO of certain group companies, for the greater good of the organization.

Top management executives must absolutely not allow their personal feelings to intrude upon their judgment with respect to medium- to long-term issues. They must be willing to learn lessons at all times and continue to refine their sensitivity to the changes occurring in society.

The following saying is found in the *Summary of Eighteen Histories*, a classic Chinese historical book:

Affairs of the times are predicted by a great man.

In other words, only a person of superior qualities can gain an insight into what needs to be done at a particular point in time. These words imply that as long as I remain at the top of our group, I must continue to make decisions in solitude by giving careful consideration to all companies within the group and their employees, and to all stakeholders associated with these companies, not to mention rewarding those officers and employees of the group companies who have worked hard to bring themselves to undertaking an IPO, yet are then told to cancel it.

4. The fourth strategy is to increase our shareholder value through mergers and acquisitions (M&A), joint ventures (JV), strategic alliances, and other means (see Exhibit 3.4).

In recent years, M&A has gained popularity, particularly among Internet-based companies. However, my advice would be to avoid hastily engaging in M&A transactions.

An empirical study conducted by Bain & Company, a leading international management consultancy, states that "75 percent of the cases involving mergers and acquisitions in the past have not resulted in the creation of corporate value." In other words, these cases have ended up as failures. While I do not think that closing a M&A deal is a particularly difficult task, speaking from my own experiences, it is extremely difficult to translate a M&A deal into an increase in shareholder value over the medium- to long-term in a formulaic fashion, such as the merger of two companies (1 + 1) creating an output of 3 or 5.

Why a Successful M&A Is Difficult to Achieve. One reason is that the actual cash flows of the acquisition target company are not consistent with the cash flows projected before the deal was closed. As a result, the rate of return on investment in the deal does not exceed the capital cost of the acquiring company. Another reason can be attributed to the difficulty arising from different corporate cultures and corporate climates be-

**Evaluation of mergers and acquisitions (M&A),
joint ventures, and strategic alliances**

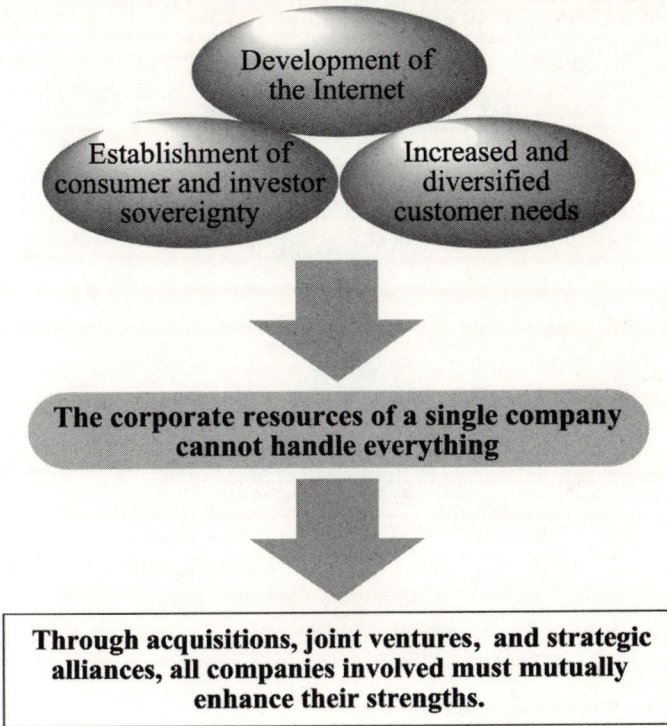

Development of
the Internet

Establishment of
consumer and investor
sovereignty

Increased and
diversified
customer needs

**The corporate resources of a single company
cannot handle everything**

**Through acquisitions, joint ventures, and strategic
alliances, all companies involved must mutually
enhance their strengths.**

EXHIBIT 3.4 Strategy to Increase Market Capitalization (2)

tween the acquiring company and the acquisition target company (see
Exhibit 3.5).

If these two different corporate cultures were not integrated successfully, then the synergetic effects that were expected prior to the
closing of the deal would not be realized. Also, such a problem may
trigger a situation wherein the key management members of an acquired company may leave the company, leading to a loss of customers, or a drop in productivity. In some cases it could even create an
internal conflict. This is where a postmerger integration process (PMIP)

──────── **Conditions that make an acquisition a success** ────────

Rate of return on investment $>$ Capital cost **1**	Enhancement of business portfolio and synergies with existing businesses **2**	Integration of corporate cultures through postmerger integration process (PMIP) **3**

It is difficult to make an acquisition a success, and it takes a while for the outcome to become obvious.

Joint ventures and strategic alliances carry less risk and are quite often more effective than acquisitions.

Examples: E*Trade, Morningstar Japan, E-LOAN, INSWEB, Gomez Consulting all started out as joint ventures.

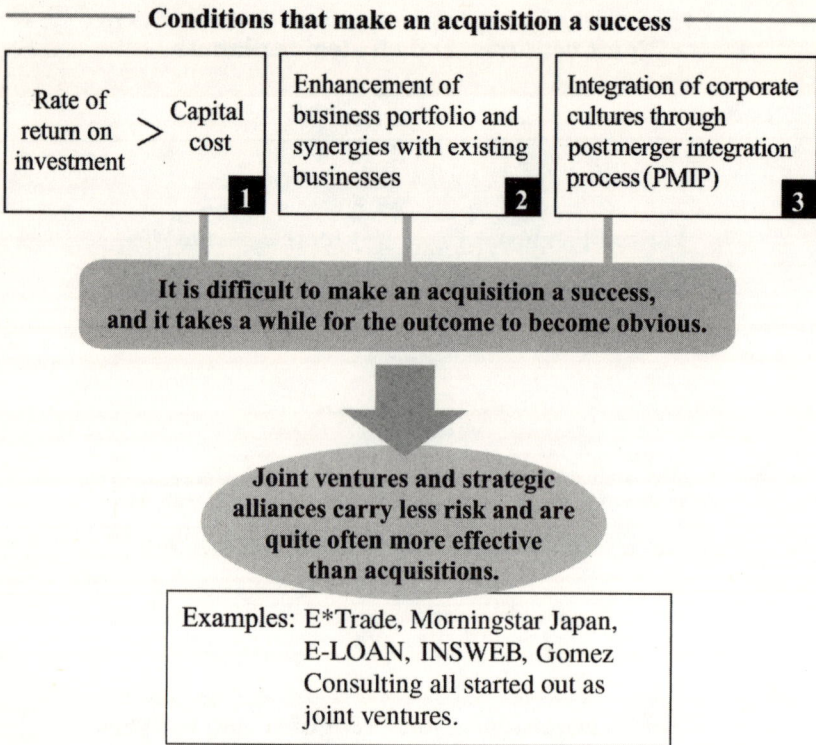

EXHIBIT 3.5   Risky Acquisition Strategy

comes into play, which is very important, to avoid the aforementioned consequences and to facilitate the smooth integration of the two companies, increase shareholder value consistently in the medium to long-term, and finally make the transaction a successful M&A in the true sense. In Japan, however, the concept of PMIP is not as widespread, so presently there are no professional corporate integration managers who are specialized in handling the nuances of these affairs.

Activities of Integration Teams in the United States. It is common in the United States that prior to the closing of an acquisition deal, an integration manager with vast experience in corporate integration matters is appointed. The integration manager will then assemble an integration team comprised of several members. Once the acquisition deal has closed, the team begins to design an integration plan with the key personnel from the acquired company. It is important that the plan is designed to establish a new management philosophy and a vision, strategies to realize the vision, and an efficient system and organizational structure to actually implement them.

When the acquired company is quite large in size, it must be realized that the required PMIP will be a huge task that could be equivalent to a corporate restructuring for both the acquiring company and the acquired company, and it is absolutely essential during the integration process that not only the top management on both sides but also their staff at every level thoroughly communicate with each other. This is indispensable because if the integration fails to progress smoothly, a situation may be triggered wherein some key employees may leave the companies or a loss of customers or shareholders may occur, eventually resulting in a significant deterioration in the corporate value of the companies involved.

Joint Ventures and Strategic Alliances. For companies that operate Internet-related businesses such as ours, joint ventures and strategic alliances are particularly effective tools for increasing shareholder value. Some of our group companies including E*Trade Japan, Morningstar Japan, and SBI VeriTrans, as well as E-LOAN and InsWeb, both of which were business divisions of Finance All, started out as joint ventures with United States companies. The amounts of capital invested in establishing these companies were quite insignificant, but a majority of them became publicly held within three to five years (see Exhibit 3.6).

In the case of Internet-related businesses, after an IPO their shares tend to be highly valued by the market, partly owing to their fast pace of growth, so their total market capitalization increases accordingly. They have much more appeal than a M&A situation as far as the rate of return on investment is concerned.

While a M&A is an excellent tool in the sense that it can save time, joint ventures fare pretty well, considering the amount of time and energy a company must spend during the PMIP. I do believe, however,

■ **E*Trade Japan K.K.**   Establishment: June 1998; First profitable year: Fiscal
                                         year ended March 2000
                                         Group's initial capital investment: Approx. 1.57 billion yen
                                         Group's initial shareholding ratio: 58%

■ **Morningstar Japan K.K.**   Establishment: March 1998; First profitable year: Fiscal
                                         year ended Dec. 1999
                                         Group's initial capital investment: Approx. 160 million yen
                                         Group's initial shareholding ratio: 40% (55.6% including
                                         warrant holding)

■ **E-LOAN Japan Co., Ltd.**   Establishment: May 1999; First profitable year: Fiscal
                                         year ended March 2001
                                         Group's initial capital investment: Approx. 300 million yen
                                         Group's initial shareholding ratio: 60%

■ **InsWeb Japan K.K.**   Establishment: Dec. 1998; First profitable year: Fiscal
                                         year ended Sept. 2000
                                         Group's initial capital investment: Approx. 360 million yen
                                         Group's initial shareholding ratio: 60%

■ **Gomez Consulting Co., Ltd.**   Establishment: March 2001; First profitable year: Fiscal
                                         year ended Dec. 2001
                                         Group's initial capital investment: Approx. 230 million yen
                                         Group's initial shareholding ratio: 65%

EXHIBIT 3.6   Joint Ventures Enable a Quick Launch of a Business on Small
Invested Capital

that a joint venture can be carried out much more smoothly under a
structure wherein one company has full command, that is to say, the
majority voting power.

Strategic alliances have been used frequently all over the world in
recent years, and they come in a variety of forms, from those without
any capital ties to those with cross-shareholding ties.

No longer capable of increasing customer satisfaction with their individual management resources due to increasingly diversified customer needs, rapid progress in the globalization of business
environments, intensified technology races, and other factors, a number of companies are now opting for strategic alliances.

Strategic alliances typically do not require a large sum of capital. There are apparently many cases in the past where they have proven to be very effective, in that not only do they achieve the strategic goals of all partners involved, but they also increase their respective corporate value. Strategic alliances are formed for a variety of reasons, such as market expansion, better customer reach, securing technology, cost reduction, better product lineup, mitigation of risk, and stronger value chain, among other things.

From a "Strong Company" to a "Strong and Respected Company"

The transformation from a "strong company" to a "strong and respected company" is a kind of paradigm shift, and we must recognize that such transformation has an enormous impact to the extent that we must alter the very basis of the conceptual framework that fundamentally governs the views and ways of thinking of all officers and employees of our group (see Exhibit 3.7).

I believe that in order to realize this paradigm shift, we will need to undergo the following processes: (1) Social Nature, (2) Trust of Society, and (3) Company Virtues (see Exhibit 3.8).

Recognizing Its Social Nature. In the first process, a company must recognize that it has a social nature. Each company owes its very existence to society, of which it is an integral member and to which it belongs. This is what makes it so important for each company to contribute to the continuance and advancement of society.

Earning the Trust of Society. In the next process, a company must earn the trust of society based on the aforesaid recognition. In order to do that, each company must clearly define what types of values, management philosophy and vision it holds, as well as what it is trying to achieve and who will benefit from such action. The company must make all of these matters known to the general public and engage in corporate activities in line with what they have defined.

Local Communities NPO · Shareholders · Business Partners

Incorporate the broader view of all stakeholders associated with the company and build better relationships with them.

"Strong and Respected Company"
· Social contribution through the primary business
· Creation of honest and fair profits
· Direct contributions to local communities
· Compliance with the law and practice of ethical behavior
· Nurturing of human resources
· Environmental consciousness

Human Capital · Customers

Increase a narrowly defined "corporate value" which assumes that there are only a limited number of stakeholders.

Government Administration · General Consumers

Strive to increase corporate value as an aggregate of customer value, shareholder value, and human capital value over the long term.

Shareholders

"Strong Company"
· High earning power
· Focus on corporate efficiency
· Maintenance of growth capabilities

Human Capital · Customers

Narrowly defined "corporate value"
= Shareholder value

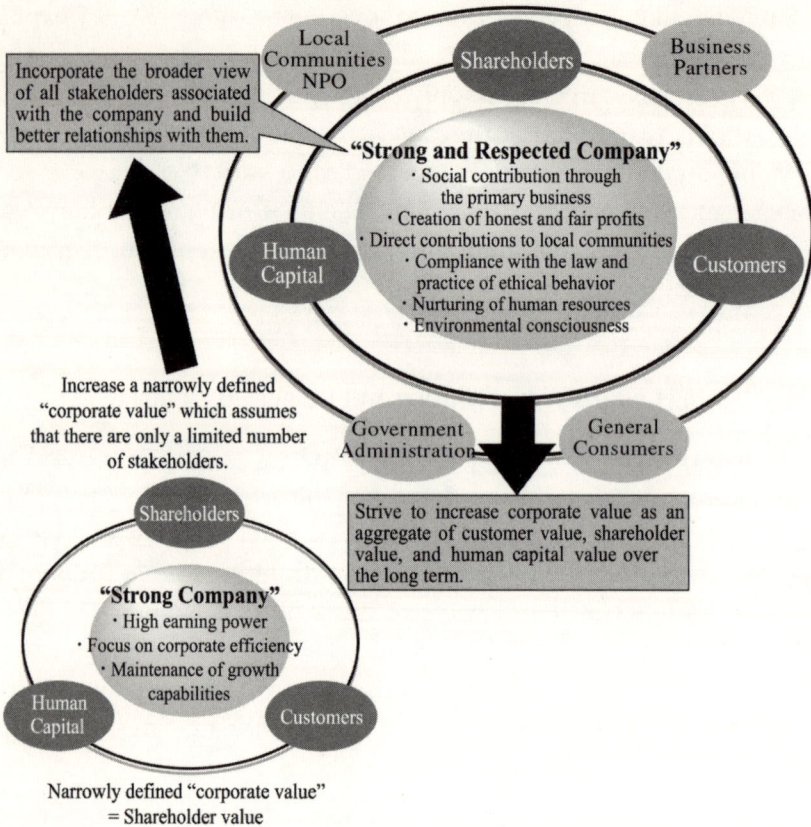

EXHIBIT 3.7   From a "Strong Company" to a "Strong and Respected Company"

To put it differently, each company must clearly set forth its conceptual framework with respect to its values, management philosophy, and corporate vision. In addition, within this framework the company must define the specific business domains in which it will operate its businesses and determine its competitive strategies, target customer segments, business portfolio, and so on.

Subsequently, all of these matters must be expressed extensively inside and outside the company in order to gain the support of people who can identify with them. The most important thing is to ensure that there will be no disagreement between what the company said it will

From a "strong company" to a "strong and respected company"

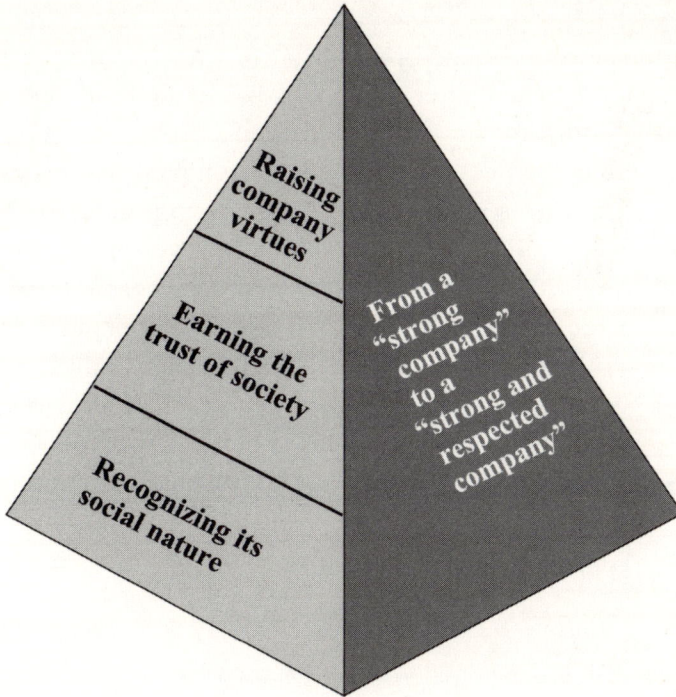

EXHIBIT 3.8   Three Processes for Realizing a Paradigm Shift

do and what it actually does. If it does this, then the company will earn the respect of its stakeholders, such as its customers, business partners, and shareholders. This means that no matter how much a company spends on advertisements, if its products and services turn out to be of poor quality, then the company will likely draw negative opinions for being all talk but no action.

In this sense, how a company's employees treat its customers becomes very important. If employees mistreat customers, then the company will be labeled insincere, and its brand image will suffer tremendously. For this reason, each company should put into place and improve upon their internal operations, training, and professional development systems.

Raising Company Virtues. The final part of the process toward the realization of the paradigm shift after a company has earned the trust of society is to raise "company virtues."

I believe that each company possesses company virtues in much the same way as a person possesses virtues. A corporate organization is also known as a "juridical person," and in the eyes of the law it is an entity that possesses rights and obligations and is deemed to possess a juridical character. In the same manner as a physical person, a corporation will be subject to harsh social sanctions when its juridical character violates social justice or fairness. Also, just as a physical person of virtue is respected by those around him or her, a corporation of virtue, that is to say, a corporation with company virtues, earns the respect of society.

In the *Great Learning*, a classic Chinese text, we find the following saying:

> The ruler will first take pains about his own virtue. Possessing virtue will give him the people. Possessing the people will give him the territory. Possessing the territory will give him its wealth. Possessing the wealth, he will have resources for expenditure.

This saying suggests that a person of virtue will naturally attract people who will allow him or her to rule their land to which wealth and resources will be naturally drawn. The person will then be able to accomplish good results for the people.

A company, which is a corporate organization, is an aggregate of people; hence, their moral character is very important. A group of people of high moral character, that is to say a company with high company virtues, should invariably prosper in business and be respected in society.

Some of my readers may be wondering why I am now bringing up a cliched and abstract ethical theory relating to company virtues.

However, building a business and managing a company are, needless to say, part of human behavior. As long as this holds true, I believe that it is quite natural for one to take the view that a company's top management executives and members of its management team should have the largest impact on the company's management policies, strategies, and accomplishments, as well as its future potential and reputation. It is absolutely necessary that a company raise the moral character of its officers and employees in order to become a respected company.

It was based on this belief that I wrote *Fuhen no Keiei, Seicho no Keiei* (*Universal Management, Growth Management*) (PHP Institute, Inc., Tokyo, 2000), *Jinbutsu wo Tsukuru* (*Developing Character*) (PHP Institute, Inc., Tokyo, 2003), and *Chugoku Koten kara Moratta "Fushigi na Chikara"* (*"Mysterious Powers" Gained from Chinese Classics*) (Mikasa Shobo Co., Ltd, Tokyo, 2005). I wrote these books in the hope that their readers would primarily be the officers and employees of the SBI Group. I had hoped that books like these (each of which includes a number of quotations from Chinese classics) would give momentum to inspiring our officers and employees to raise their moral character. Of course, it would be more than I could dream of if these books are read openly by the general public, as it may offer many Japanese people the chance to become familiar with the Chinese classics as we were in the old days, and encourage them to make an effort to continuously improve their overall character.

Another Chinese classic, *The Book of Changes* (*I Ching*), contains the following saying:

> The superior man, in accordance with this, stores largely in his memory the words and deeds of former men, to subserve the accumulation of his virtue.

This means that a wise person learns the words and acts of sages, and uses them as a foundation for developing his or her own virtues.

Now let's elaborate a little further on the practical activities undertaken to achieve higher company virtues.

One activity is to ensure that all officers and employees of a company raise their moral character and maintain appropriate ethical values. To do this, it is extremely important for a company to have in place systems for hiring, assessing, and recruiting human capital with a focus on "virtue" rather than "aptitude."

Another activity is to maintain and continuously improve the trust of society that the company has earned. In other words, the company should establish and maintain a strong corporate brand. A corporate brand is created when a company positions all of its product lines under one umbrella and projects a single image that represents these product lines. In their scholarly article, "Are the Strategic Stars Aligned for Your Corporate Brand?," in the *Harvard Business Review*, February 2001, Professor Mary Jo Hatch of the University of Virginia and Professor Majken Shultz of the Copenhagen Business School argue that in order to create a strong corporate brand a company must align three fundamental elements, namely "vision," "culture," and "image," which must interact with one another.

The word "image" used here refers to the overall impression of a company held by third parties. Third parties include all the stakeholders in a company: its customers, shareholders, the media, the general public, and so on. The authors of the article refer to the aforementioned three fundamental elements as "strategic stars." They argue that it is insufficient when only two of the three stars are harmonized and that a company needs to have a corporate culture that can support its vision and raise its credibility.

The authors also remark, "While corporate vision and strategies are themselves powerful strategic tools, once they are aligned with stakeholder images, the corporate brand can become a powerhouse." In my opinion, we could also combine vision with corporate culture, add to that corporate social contribution activities, then collectively refer to these as a "corporate personality." This is because, as stated by the authors, "together, they (vision and corporate culture) are a powerful tool in helping you stand out from your competition."

My own take on this matter is that the alignment of a corporate personality and the image of a company is the key to its corporate brand. The company must ensure that there is no gap between the two at any given time.

Furthermore, making sure that there is no gap alone is insufficient. In order to project a good image, a company should maintain a harmony with all of its stakeholders and maintain as well as improve the social nature with which it has been credited in its business activities. In addition, the company must aggressively promote the making of donations, volunteer activities, corporate philanthropy, and other direct social contribution activities. Once the company is able to develop and maintain its corporate brand, it will naturally continue to be highly regarded in its primary businesses.

Through the practical activities described here and a long succession of efforts, a company must prove that its growth can contribute to the advancement of society. To be able to earn the trust and respect of society, the company needs to make steady and continuous efforts. As such, this goal cannot possibly be achieved overnight.

Four Strategies for Realizing the SBI Group's Vision

FURTHER DEVELOPMENT OF THE BUSINESS ECOSYSTEM THROUGH EXPANSION INTO NEW BUSINESS FIELDS

I believe that to allow our existing business ecosystem to achieve an efficient and dramatic growth, we must implement two primary measures.

First, we must facilitate the self-advancement and self-growth of our business ecosystem by exhaustively pursuing the synergies existing among the various companies comprising the ecosystem. Secondly, we must ensure the growth of our business ecosystem by assimilating external management resources into the SBI Group in order to allow for an immediate expansion of the ecosystem, while seeking to generate synergies between new and existing management resources. We cannot choose to implement only one of these two measures, as they must be implemented in tandem.

Keep in mind that neither of the two measures will work effectively if the ecosystem has not advanced to a certain level of maturity; if the situation is otherwise, then sufficient synergies cannot be generated among the companies that comprise the ecosystem. To illustrate this point, let's look at one example—the synergies between SBI E*TRADE SECURITIES and SBI Asset Management.

Self-Advancement of the Business Ecosystem Through Pursuit of Synergies

SBI E*TRADE SECURITIES Co., Ltd. currently boasts more than 1,290,000 securities accounts, which are held by various types of customers. To meet the diversified needs of its customers, SBI E*TRADE SECURITIES has offered a wide range of products. The company has sold in excess of 7 billion yen in shares of the SBI Private Equity Fund III created by SBI Asset Management Co., Ltd. The fund owed its impressive sales results not only to the depth of SBI E*TRADE SECURITIES, but also significantly to the exceptionally favorable track record of similar funds previously offered for subscription by SBI Asset Management.

The final redemption price per unit of the Softbank Private Equity Fund, which was launched in July 2000 is 21,742 yen (redemption date: March 3, 2006; the base price based on 10,000 yen invested on July 18, 2000), and also the final redemption price per unit for what was launched in June 2001 is 19,660 yen (redemption date: October 12, 2005; the base price based on 10,000 yen invested on June 29, 2001). As can be seen, these funds have been redeemed with very favorable performance returns. The main driver of this is that SBI Asset Management possesses a business base that makes it possible for the funds to produce high investment yields.

As demonstrated in this example, the synergies existing among various companies can be mutually generated only if customer and business bases have been formed at a level that is considered more than adequate.

Further Expansion of the Existing Business Ecosystem with External Management Resources

The second measure involves the assimilation of external management resources. At the SBI Group, there are four resource categories:

1. Financial business fields that can generate synergies with the majority of existing SBI Group companies.

2. Nonfinancial fields where some SBI Group companies have customer bases that overlap with the customer segments of other companies.
3. Development of our existing financial businesses globally.
4. Expansion into new business fields.

Now let me explain these resource categories one by one in further detail using examples.

Financial Business Fields

Banking. Banking is the field into which I am seriously considering undertaking a full-fledged entry.

I am aware that banking is a fairly tough business. My decision to foray into banking has come after studying and analyzing, in my own way, the past and present circumstances of U.S. banks, for instance, how they were swept up in the asset-inflation bubble in commercial real estate in the late 1980s only to be subsequently dealt a heavy blow in the face of the bursting of the bubble. I have also studied how the environment surrounding Japanese banks has changed since the 1990s to date. While in a sense U.S. banks have made a full-fledged recovery since the late 1990s, their Japanese counterparts appear to have come only halfway through.

The loan margins of Japanese banks are very thin; I believe they are roughly one-third to a half of what banks in the United States and Europe earn. It will be difficult to improve these low margins unless Japanese banks accurately gain a grasp of the relationship that exists between lending risk and return and charge high margins on loans that are risky, as U.S. and European banks do. In addition, Japanese banks do not earn adequate revenues from fees and commission from other services to make up for the low margins on their loans.

You may wonder why very little attention has been paid to this problem, which is fundamental to banks. I think that the main reasons are the historical cost-based accounting system used by banks and unrealized gains from high stock prices on the equity security holdings held by banks over a long period of time.

In the calculation of a bank capital ratio in accordance with the rules set forth and introduced by the Bank for International Settlements (BIS) in 1988, the Ministry of Finance allowed up to 45 percent of unrealized gains on stock holdings to be included in capital. Therefore, Japanese banks had neglected to make an effort to boost their Tier 1 capital (shareholders' equity and debenture-type preferred securities issued through subsidiaries), which in principle is the core capital of banks. I believe that the fact that banks neglected to maintain an adequate capital had significantly raised the magnitude of the problem of their nonperforming loans in the 1990s. While Japanese banks began to fairly aggressively dispose of their stock holdings after the bursting of the economic bubble, it was a little too late by that time.

Japanese banks also have a low rate of return on their bond trading activities. This has very much to do with the fact that the Japanese government's postwar financial administration has consistently centered on indirect financing. As a result, the Japanese bond market lacks depth, which makes it difficult to build and manage a sound bond portfolio.

Pure-Play Internet Banks. Given the problem of low profitability that is faced by Japanese banks and the historical and customary elements that have created the problem, I could not help but hesitate in making an entry into banking during the very early stages of the SBI Group. So I decided instead to gain some experience in banking by taking an approach that one might describe as a rather low-key approach. In April 2000, I entered the field of banking in the form of the Softbank Branch of Suruga Bank. In August 2001, the branch reported its first profit on a monthly basis and by March 2002 had achieved a profit on a full-year basis.

In the half-year period ended September 2002, we started to split profits equally with Suruga Bank based on a profit sharing scheme. Since then the branch has steadily increased its profits. While this business is doing well, our presence in the banking industry in the form of a branch such as this is nothing more than part of our preparation and lesson–learning for a full-scale entry into the banking business in the future.

I usually make preparations and do a lot of studying in a meticulous fashion before venturing into any new business. I quite often use the "hypothesis and test" technique, which is talked about by Mr. Toshifumi Suzuki, the chairman of Seven & i Holdings Co., Ltd. (formerly Ito Yokado).

I began to study pure-play Internet banks in 1995, or around that time, through our investments in several Internet-based banks in the United States. As was the case for Internet-based securities firms, a number of Internet-based banks in the United States were created but within three to four years their fates ended up in one of the following three scenarios: Some were acquired by major banks; some, like CompuBank, simply went bankrupt; and some, like Telebank, were acquired by Internet-based securities firms.

Discovery of the Synergistic Effect between Internet-Based Securities Firms and Banks. The most significant reason why Internet-based banks did not thrive was this: Although these banks were able to attract deposits by offering high deposit rates, they found it difficult to invest deposited funds at interest rates higher than their deposit rates. Every time I saw or heard about the disastrous status of Internet-based banks in the United States, I reminded myself that I would have to be extra careful in making a full-fledged entry into the Internet banking business. That is why I made sure that the Softbank Branch of Suruga Bank would be operated jointly by Suruga Bank and our group as a separate and independent business within Suruga Bank. Through this business I have very carefully studied the synergies created between Internet-based securities firms and banks.

The bottom line is that there is a larger synergistic effect between Internet-based securities firms and banks than between other businesses. In the case of the Softbank Branch of Suruga Bank, nearly 60 percent of the customers who opened accounts with the branch between October 2004 and March 2005 were also SBI E*TRADE SECURITIES customers.

This is largely explained by the fact that the branch offers several preferred services that are available only to SBI E*TRADE SECURITIES customers. For example, the branch offers an instant credit service for the settlement of securities transactions (real-time fund transfers with no fund transfer fee charged). It also offers several services that benefit the customers of both SBI E*TRADE SECURITIES and the branch, such as no fees for fund withdrawals from ATM machines, discount fees for fund transfers to other banks, and a 1 percent discount on unsecured loan rates. The offering of these special services has propelled the Softbank Branch into the top position among all Suruga Bank branches in terms of percentage growth in the number of customers.

Bringing Synergies Into Action Within a Business Ecosystem. Keep in mind that the fact these synergies can be generated alone would not convince me to make a decision to venture into the banking business, especially now that small- to medium-sized banks have lost their appeal in terms of profitability, as I mentioned earlier. Then, what would I need to convince myself? It would be too difficult for banks to cover huge IT-related costs and still end up with a reasonable amount of profit simply by increasing the number of their customer accounts.

I would say that we should give up the idea of expanding into banking altogether, unless we can bring synergies into action through interaction with other member companies of our business ecosystem. Luckily for us, the SBI Group is capable of creating synergies between banks and various companies within and outside the SBI Group. These companies possess good growth potential, are also investees in various funds offered by SBI Investment, and would make desirable borrowers for bank loans. For example, these group companies include SBI Mortgage Co., Ltd., with 237.8 billion yen in housing loan balances as of August 31, 2006, SBI Equal Credit Co., Ltd., which specializes in consumer and small business finance, and SBI Partners Co., Ltd. (merged into SBI Holdings, Inc. in March 2006), which operates a real estate business. I have formed the expectation that, from the perspective of the overall group, the synergies to be created by these companies will produce a very positive outcome worthy of our entry into banking. Needless to say, we will have to come up with very innovative ideas as to what method we should use for our entry into banking.

To sum up, based on the significant synergies with our Internet-based securities business, an Internet bank must pursue synergies through interaction with the various other existing companies that comprise the business ecosystem. Only after this task has been completed will an Internet bank be able to produce profits and make a positive contribution to the overall group.

Nonfinancial Business Fields

Real Estate. An example of the second resource category is the real estate business. Most people who own real estate properties that are not used as their residence, also own marketable securities, such as stocks and bonds. In other words, it is a common practice among the well-to-do population to invest their assets in a diversified portfolio that contains several types of financial products, real estate, and the like, based on their risk and return, and liquidity. Therefore, there is a certain area in this industry where the customer base of SBI Partners (merged into SBI Holdings, Inc. in March 2006), which operates a real estate business, overlaps with the high net worth customer base of SBI E*TRADE SECURITIES. In addition, it is possible to allow SBI E*TRADE SECURITIES and SBI Securities to solicit subscriptions to the real estate funds and real estate investment trusts (REITs) formed by SBI Partners, another group company.

Global Development of Existing Financial Businesses

Examples for this category include the conversion of E*Trade Korea into a subsidiary of SBI E*TRADE SECURITIES and the formation of an alliance with E*Trade Financial in the United States. Another example is the alliance between SBI Holdings and Kingsway in Hong Kong, which also includes the formation of a capital tie-up. A series of these global-scale alliances that includes capital tie-ups are making it possible for customers of SBI E*TRADE SECURITIES to trade U.S. stocks, Hong Kong and Chinese stocks (H stocks), and Korean stocks from their personal computers in Japan.

Going forward, we will work at enabling customers to trade stocks online in a wide range of countries through the global network of U.S.-based E*Trade Financial (see Exhibit 4.1). If we can succeed in this task, then it will be a huge push in differentiating ourselves from our competitors, as there are no companies at this moment that can provide such service. In addition, making it possible to trade through various stock markets across the globe, we will be able to accomplish global asset allocation (the global allocation of assets through investments in stocks in various countries) in a genuine sense. This means that customers will be able to make investment decisions based on

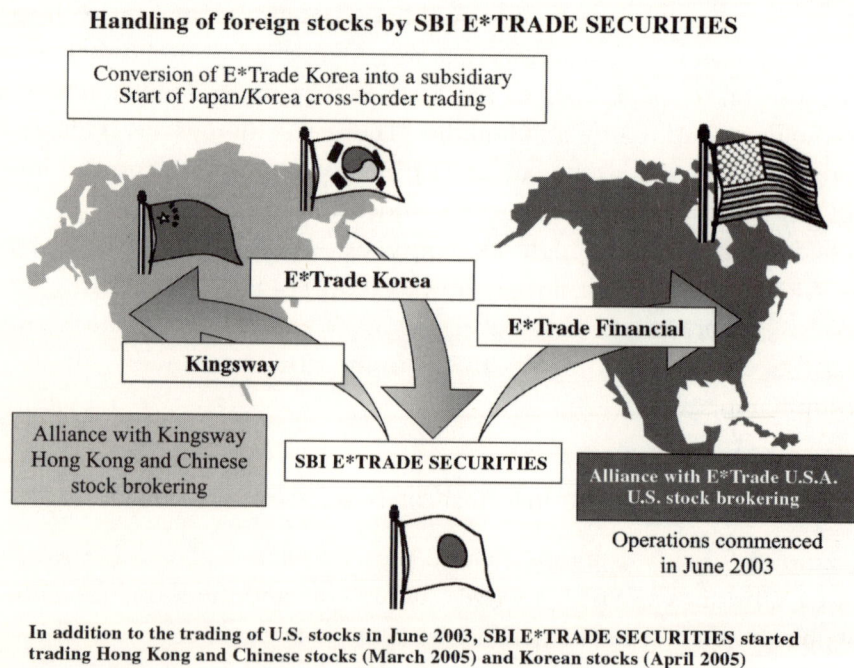

Handling of foreign stocks by SBI E*TRADE SECURITIES

Conversion of E*Trade Korea into a subsidiary
Start of Japan/Korea cross-border trading

E*Trade Korea

E*Trade Financial

Kingsway

Alliance with Kingsway Hong Kong and Chinese stock brokering

SBI E*TRADE SECURITIES

Alliance with E*Trade U.S.A. U.S. stock brokering

Operations commenced in June 2003

In addition to the trading of U.S. stocks in June 2003, SBI E*TRADE SECURITIES started trading Hong Kong and Chinese stocks (March 2005) and Korean stocks (April 2005)

EXHIBIT 4.1 Global Asset Allocation

economic and relative foreign exchange conditions in various countries in the world, as well as the market conditions in each country, regardless of time zone.

Expansion into New Business Fields

When we speak of expanding into new business fields, we mean to make an entry into new business fields using our core financial businesses. To be specific, there are two cases in which we can do this. The first case involves making an entry into new business fields that can generate significant synergies within existing SBI Group companies. In the other case, we can make a foray into new business fields in which existing SBI Group companies could apply their business models without making any modifications.

An example of the first case is Nexyz. Trade Inc., a securities brokerage joint venture between Nexyz. Corporation and SBI E*TRADE SECURITIES. Nexyz. Trade makes full use of the telemarketing, direct-mail marketing, and other marketing know-how of Nexyz. Corporation in order to seek to increase the number of accounts among wealth holders who do not normally engage in the Internet-based trading of securities. Another example of this case is the business alliance between Autobytel Japan K.K. and Finance All Corporation (merged into SBI Holdings, Inc. in March 2006). Through this alliance, Finance All offers a comprehensive auto insurance quote service to the customers of Autobytel Japan, and SBI Holdings holds nearly 11 percent of the shares of Autobytel, making it the third-largest shareholder.

A good example of the second case is Finance All's move into the operation of comprehensive comparison web sites. Finance All applies its business model and know-how to other nonfinancial fields, which it has learned through its marketplace business based on insurance and loan product comparison web sites, for instance, websites that provide comprehensive relocation cost quotations and remodeling cost comparisons.

Through our entry into new business fields utilizing the forms just described, we will seek to further expand and advance the business ecosystem of our group.

STRENGTHENING OF A CORPORATE COMMUNICATION (CC) STRATEGY

Corporate identity (CI) strategies were actively adopted by U.S. companies during the 1960s as a means for improving their corporate image. A CI strategy clearly sets forth and makes known, both within and outside a company, what the company does and what goals it is working toward, as well as its identity and characteristics. Depending upon its nature, a CI strategy was also used to improve the reputation and credibility of a company among consumers and local communities, as well as to motivate its employees and raise their sense of belonging to the company. In the 1990s, the term CI began to lose its popularity; instead, this idea gradually evolved into a brand strategy and a strategy for strengthening corporate communications with society in a broad sense. Today, it takes the form of a corporate communication (CC) strategy.

Let us have a brief look at the CC strategy of the SBI Group. Of course, I should mention that when I founded the group in 1999, I could not afford to spare much time in thinking about a CC strategy. My efforts in this department went only as far as reading a few books about branding and having only vague ideas about it.

Changes in the CC Strategy of the SBI Group

I may say that the CC strategy of the SBI Group has gradually increased in sophistication, as the degree of maturity of our business development activities has increased. To illustrate this change, let us look at our brand strategy in chronological order. In the beginning, we simply established companies whose names began with the name of the parent company, "SOFTBANK," such as Softbank Finance and Softbank Investment. We did this simply because we were wholly owned by Softbank at that time, and we thought we should take advantage of the name recognition of the parent.

Then, we established a series of joint ventures with U.S. companies for the purpose of facilitating a speedy expansion of our businesses and introducing an innovative business model to our group. The names of the joint ventures established in these early days carried the names of our U.S. partners. Both E*Trade Japan and Morningstar Japan fit this case. It made sense for these two companies to bear the U.S. partners' names because they had already been highly regarded as internationally known brands within and outside the U.S. Over time, we no longer formed any joint ventures with U.S. companies, but instead we formed new companies ourselves, or joint ventures were set up with other Japanese companies. As a result, we assigned unique names that could better personify their lines of business.

For example, Good Mortgage Corporation (currently SBI Mortgage Co.,, Ltd.) provides housing loans, and Web-Lease Co., Ltd, (currently SBI Lease Co., Ltd.) provides leases.

Up to this point, each group company, under its own unique company name and brand image, worked hard to gain recognition and raise its brand power. However, with the birth of SBI Holdings, Inc., which is a pure holding company, on July 1, 2005, we established a unified brand for the SBI Group (see Exhibit 4.2).

In line with the introduction of the new unified brand, we decided to change the company names of a number of our group companies to bear the name "SBI." Going forward, I hold the expectation that as each group company faces various markets as an "SBI" company, the SBI brand will very rapidly penetrate into these markets and gain increasing recognition. As a result, the impact of the SBI brand's appeal to customers will likely improve for the products and services offered by each group company (see Exhibit 4.3).

To clearly establish the group identity, the name of each subsidiary will bear the "SBI" corporate brand, which is increasingly recognized as an advanced financial group, and each operating company will take advantage of the SBI brand value to maximize the group's corporate value.

The unified brand will serve as the cohesive power in group management and will generate a sense of solidarity and unity through the sharing of the brand value.

SBI Group's unified brand logo

Description of logo design:

The dignified and steadfast "SBI" letters represent the group's confidence in meeting customer and social expectations. The letters are italicized in order to visualize movement and represent group innovation and growth.

The arch represents a dynamic network and the creation of new value through group company collaboration and synergies.

The logo colors are SBI blue and SBI red. SBI blue represents reason and the ability to make accurate, composed decisions. SBI red (arch) represents the passion to create a new future for the financial services industry.

EXHIBIT 4.2   Establishment of the SBI Group's Unified Brand

Background of the Establishment and Promotion of the SBI Brand

The only way to turn the SBI brand into a powerful driver that can increase the corporate value of the SBI Group is to continuously undertake a hardworking effort. While this is true, it is certainly important for each group to engage in CC activities in a strategic manner. As the chief executive officer (CEO) of the SBI Group, I decided that the group would give its highest priority to the establishment of a powerful SBI brand as early as possible and that I myself would spearhead this task.

Before

Under its own unique company name and brand image, each group company efficiently undertakes business activities.

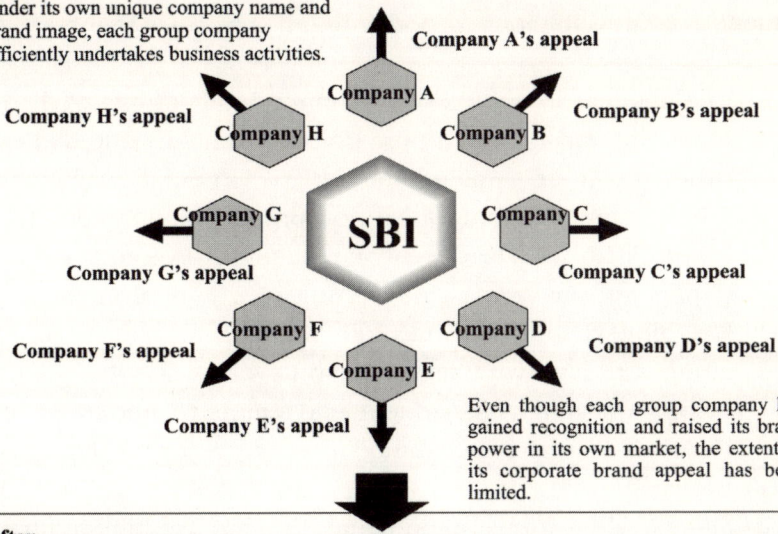

Company H's appeal

Company A's appeal

Company B's appeal

Company G's appeal

Company C's appeal

Company F's appeal

Company D's appeal

Company E's appeal

Company A
Company H
Company B
SBI
Company G
Company C
Company F
Company D
Company E

Even though each group company has gained recognition and raised its brand power in its own market, the extent of its corporate brand appeal has been limited.

After

Each group company undertakes business activities with the "SBI" DNA both in name and in substance.

SBI appeal

Strengthening of brand power

Strengthening of brand power

SBI appeal

SBI

SBI appeal

Strengthening of brand power

Strengthening of brand power

SBI appeal

As each group company faces various markets as an "SBI" company, the SBI brand will very rapidly penetrate into these markets. Using the high visibility of the SBI brand as a weapon, each group can create a strong and broader appeal.

EXHIBIT 4.3   Impact of the SBI Group's Unified Brand Appeal

You may be wondering why I decided to make such a strong commitment to establishing our corporate brand. There are four reasons.

1. The first reason has to do with timing. At that time, we had just made the transition to a pure holding company and had established the group's unified brand logo. Around the same period, a hostile takeover bid for Nippon Broadcasting System, Inc. by Livedoor Co., Ltd. made daily headlines on TV and in the newspapers and magazines. As a result of my involvement in this bid, all of a sudden names like Softbank Investment and SBI, along with my own name, were on everybody's lips. As I look back, we would have had to spend a massive amount of advertising to gain the recognition that we received through this event.

2. Second, the various brand names that are used in the financial services provided by our SBI Group companies do not even serve the most basic functions that are expected of them. For example, in an age where we no longer see marked differences even between so-called "mega" banks in terms of the services and products they offer, it becomes quite meaningless to make sure that brands communicate to consumers that they are different from others, although that is what brands are expected to do.

   Furthermore, as a result of the series of mergers and industry realignments that have occurred in recent years in banking and in life and nonlife insurance industries, many companies have undergone a number of name changes, only to leave consumers so confused that they find it hard to recognize brands. As a result, brands are no longer able to serve their most basic functions.

   Against this background, financial products are becoming increasingly sophisticated and complex, while, in contrast, the ability of consumers to evaluate products is on the decline. I believe that at a time like this it becomes more important for the SBI Group to make sure that the SBI brand can play the roles originally expected of it in each capacity that it provides, as well as to ensure that the SBI brand will secure its competitive advantage.

3. Third, as part of the SBI Group's vision, we are seeking to realize a substantial increase in our shareholder value over the next three years. My thoughts are that the establishment and preservation of a powerful corporate brand will be indispensable in achieving such a goal.

   Having given a lot of thought to what a corporate brand consists of, I have concluded that there are two sides to any corporate brand. On one side, a company's corporate brand projects its values, management philosophy, vision, and all corporate activities of the company. To put it more simply, a corporate brand projects the corporate personality of a company in a condensed form. On the other side, a corporate brand represents the corporate image of a company.

   Therefore, to establish a powerful corporate brand we must narrow the gap between the corporate personality and the corporate image of that company as much as possible. Once a powerful brand has been established, the company can enhance its customer value, which will lead to an increase in sales and profits. Eventually shareholder value will increase.

   Moreover, an increase in a company's profits usually leads to an increase in remuneration to its officers and employees, while an increase in the company's share price can give zest to stock options, raising its human capital value. Once the company's brand power has strengthened, the three components of corporate value—customer value, shareholder value, and human capital value—will increase in a chain reaction and enter into a positive growth cycle through which its corporate value will improve dramatically (see Exhibit 4.4).

4. Finally, establishing a powerful corporate brand is likely to greatly assist in raising the cohesive power of the group.

   At the SBI Group, we have taken the view that it is more important to raise group value than to help our group companies

go public. It is true that having a number of our group companies turn into publicly held companies also raises some questions from the perspective of the cohesive power of the group,
because we would eventually face the problem of how the
overall group management could reflect the views of the minority shareholders in each publicly held group company, and
how to maintain a balance between the view of these minority
shareholders and the overall group management. Therefore, it
is very important to undertake efforts to raise the cohesive
power of the group through various mechanisms and methods. The awareness that various group companies share our
corporate brand can foster a sense of unity among all group
companies.

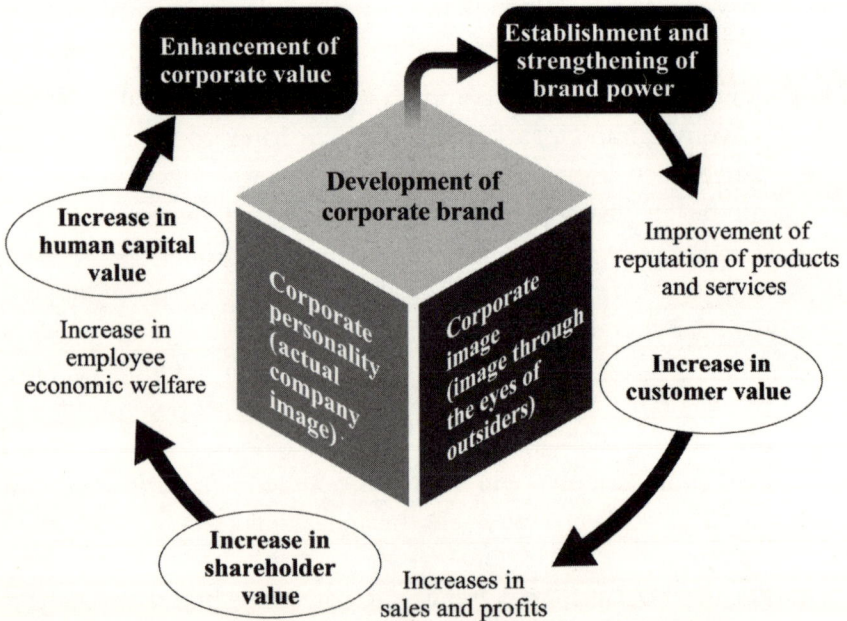

EXHIBIT 4.4 Strengthening of Corporate Brand and Enhancement of
Corporate Value

Recent CC Activities of the SBI Group

With only some forethought, I set out to build a proactive communications exchange with shareholders that would prepare us to handle more stringent investor regulations, the increasing "borderlessness" of our investor base, as well as improvements in communication technology. As part of this program, I instituted the following measures to evolve our corporate communications:

- *Business strategy meetings.* We hold business strategy meetings once a year for 500 to 600 participants, including members of the media, analysts, business partners, and companies in which we invest, among others. At the meetings we explain the strategies and business standing of the group.
- *Information meetings (information sessions for investors).* As a place to carry on direct discussions with individual shareholders, we hold meetings to discuss the SBI Group's strategy and business standing in several major cities in Japan. In May 2006, we held information meetings in Tokyo, Yokohama, Nagoya, Osaka, and Fukuoka, at which a total of more than 5,000 people participated.

    At least twice a year (after the announcement of full-year financial results and semiannual results), we meet with a number of analysts and institutional investors, including those overseas, to discuss financial standings, business progress, and future developments. In May 2006, we held an IR meeting over three days where we met with nearly 45 institutional investors.
- *Launch of the "SBI Channel" for video clip distribution.* As a part of the SBI Group's activities to promote communication, we established a corner to deliver television-quality video clips of group-related news and service information on the SBI web site.
- *Adoption of a celebrity spokesperson for the SBI Group.* We chose Mikoto Inoue as a highly visible celebrity spokesperson for the SBI Group, and she had been actively involved in the promotional activities undertaken by each group company.

Creation of a Well-Built Corporate Culture

In Japan, it appears that interest in the theory of corporate culture began to rise between 1982 and 1983. One of the factors that triggered such interest was probably the publication of several U.S. management theory books that were translated and introduced to the Japanese market. These books include *Excellent Company* by T. J. Peters and R. H. Waterman (translated by Kenichi Ohmae, Eiji Press Inc., Tokyo, 2003), and *Corporate Culture* by T. E. Deal and A. A. Kennedy (translated by Saburo Shiroyama, Iwanami Shoten Publishers, Tokyo, 1997). In the United States, ever since these books were featured as the cover story of *BusinessWeek* in the late summer of 1980, the term "corporate culture" has been frequently mentioned in discussions and debates relating to management issues.

The definition of "corporate culture" varies slightly from one business economist to another, but largely it is defined as follows:

"Corporate culture" is the unique value system and customs that are shared by all members comprising a corporate organization.—Kokusai Keiei to Kigyo Bunka (Global Management and Corporate Culture) by Takashi Nemoto and Yoko Yoshimoto Tyrefors, Gakubunsha Co., Ltd., Tokyo, 1994

Corporate culture is the collective term for the values and standards which a company created and has firmly established within the company. A corporate culture is composed of three elements: the management principles, corporate philosophy and other values of a company, which is a corporate body; socially accepted organizational codes including traditions, rituals, customs, established practices, etc.; and the ways of thinking and manners of action that are shared by all employees.—Kigyo Bunka no Kakushin to Sozo (Creation and Transformation of Corporate Culture) by Tadashi Umezawa, Yuhikaku Publishing Co., Ltd., Tokyo, 1990

A company's corporate culture is a shared system of values, assumptions, and beliefs among a firm's employees that provides guidance on how to think, perceive, and act. Because of its pronounced effect on employee behavior and effectiveness, companies increasingly recognize that corporate culture can set them apart from competitors.— *Strategy: A View from the Top* by Cornelis A. de Kluyver and John A. Pearce II (Prentice Hall, Upper Saddle River, NJ, 2002).

About 1985 top management executives in Japan became aware of corporate culture as a management issue and began to address its significance and consequence, as seen in the words of Hideo Sugiura, the former chairman of Honda Motor Co., Ltd.: "A corporate culture can be viewed as the fifth management resource that should be added to the four main management resources recognized in conventional modern management—human capital, goods, money, and information."

Process of Creating a Corporate Culture

Next, let us think about how a corporate culture as previously defined is formed. In the case of a company with a relatively short history since its establishment, it is common that the founder's values, ways of thinking, and manners of action are carried on, emulated, and shared by the officers and employees of the company. In particular, if such practice has resulted in an improved business performance and has led to a high rate of growth, then the company will likely form a kind of corporate culture.

Then, what about a company with a long history since its foundation? In this case, it is an important duty of top management executives to make over the existing corporate culture and create a new one, if the existing corporate culture can no longer be carried on, take root, or be strengthened within the company, or cannot adapt to environmental changes. The top management executives in each generation must remember two important points in order to ensure that their corporate culture will be carried on, take root, and be strengthened within the company.

1. The top management executives must carefully examine whether the corporate culture of the company is consistent with

its corporate strategies and adaptive to various environments. If he or she neglects to undertake such careful examination and implement a drastic makeover when such is called for, then it is very likely that the stronger the company's corporate culture is, the more negative its impact will become.

2. It is necessary to have various well-timed structures and systems in place. For example, we can think of the personnel and compensation system relating to, in particular, employee performance evaluations and the criteria for selecting management members (officers and leaders). In fact, the aspects highly regarded or subject to chastisement by a company, in a sense, hint at the corporate culture of that company.

It is also important to design an education and training system for professional development. A company must train its employees not only to provide them with business and specialized knowledge; it must also thoroughly educate and train its employees from the time they are hired in regard to the company's history, values, management philosophy, management policies, and so on. Through such education and training, the sense of belonging and loyalty to a company can be shared among its officers and employees, and their uniformity is also heightened.

As a result, the company's officers and employees will begin to notice "This is what our company is about" or "This is how we do things around here, " clearly distinguishing the company from other companies. Outsiders, too, will begin to say, "This is how things are carried out at that company." As a result, a company's corporate culture is expressly reflected not only in the corporate behavior of that company, but also in the behavior and attitudes of its officers and employees.

Relationship between a Corporate Culture and Long-Term Business Performance

I now touch upon whether a company's corporate culture as previously discussed has an effect on the long-term business performance of that company. According to *Corporate Culture and Performance* by

John P. Kotter and James L. Heskett (translated by Hiroyoshi Umezu, Diamond, Inc., Tokyo, 1994), the results of a study involving 207 large U.S. companies in 22 different industries over an 11-year period ending in 1990 revealed that corporate culture can have a large impact on corporate business results in the long run.

Kotter states that it is very clear that the leaders of companies, from managers at all levels, possessing cultures that emphasize all the key managerial constituencies (customers, stockholders, and employees) outperformed those firms that did not share the same cultural traits, by a huge margin (see Exhibit 4.5). A number of business economists

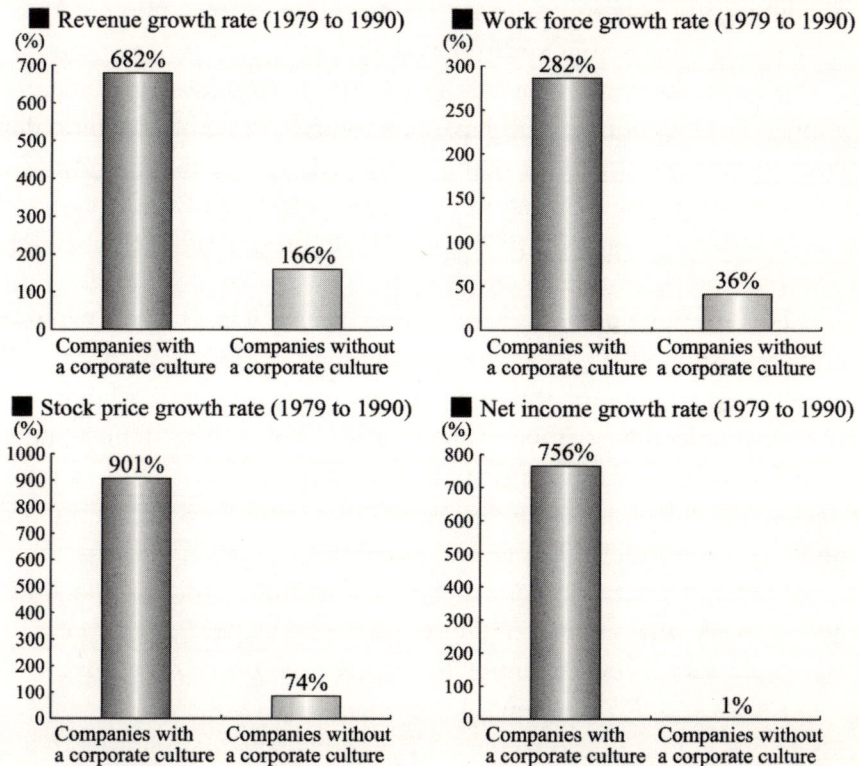

■ Revenue growth rate (1979 to 1990)

682% — Companies with a corporate culture
166% — Companies without a corporate culture

■ Work force growth rate (1979 to 1990)

282% — Companies with a corporate culture
36% — Companies without a corporate culture

■ Stock price growth rate (1979 to 1990)

901% — Companies with a corporate culture
74% — Companies without a corporate culture

■ Net income growth rate (1979 to 1990)

756% — Companies with a corporate culture
1% — Companies without a corporate culture

EXHIBIT 4.5 Companies with a Corporate Culture versus Companies with No (or a Weak) Corporate Culture

Source: Corporate Culture and Performance, John P. Kotter and James L. Heskett (Diamond, Inc., Tokyo, 1994).

other than Kotter have also acknowledged that companies with a well-built corporate culture are likely to succeed.

It is my idea that the SBI Group must also create and nurture a well-built corporate culture in order to realize a continual organizational growth and development. In just six years since its establishment, the SBI Group has expanded at a very rapid pace. Over this six-year period, our employees have grown quickly from just 55 to nearly 1,200 (as of the end of March 2006). The growth in our workforce has entirely come from the recruitment of mid-career individuals who already possess established records of employment. As the size of the businesses of the group has grown very rapidly, we have recruited individuals, primarily from various financial institutions, who could instantly play an important part in our workforce.

This suggests that a majority of the SBI Group's human capital are comprised of individuals who have previously worked under different corporate cultures for more than 10 years. Given such a situation, I have undertaken continual efforts as a representative of the SBI Group to create a unique and well-built corporate culture. Writing books such as this one is a part of these efforts.

This is my seventh book, and I would really like the officers and employees of the SBI Group, more than anyone else, to read it. I say this because I want them, through this book, to understand, digest, and share corporate management values, a code of ethics, management policies, and so on, from my point of view as head of the SBI Group. It is also part of the aforementioned efforts that I give a speech at the beginning of each month during our morning gatherings, and assemble the management team members for management strategy meetings where I voice my opinions. I also personally interview all of our prospective employees in order to distinguish those who share our group values and management philosophy.

The SBI Group began to recruit new university graduates in 2005, and we welcomed some 40 new employees in the spring of 2006. Of course, I personally met with all of them during the final round of interviews and informally accepted their employment. These individuals, chosen from more than 1,400 applicants, are certainly quite excellent in terms of their personality and skills. I am now seriously considering how we should nurture and foster them. I hope that by continuing to recruit new graduates for the next 10 years or so we will be able to firmly establish a unique and well-built corporate culture that will certainly become a significant asset for the SBI Group.

The *Guan Zi*, a collection of ancient Chinese writings, contains the following saying:

> *If you plan for a year, plant a seed.*
> *If for ten years, plant a tree.*
> *If for a hundred years, teach the people.*
> *When you sow a seed once, you will reap a single harvest.*
> *When you teach the people, you will reap a hundred harvests.*

This saying suggests that if one forms a plan for an entire life, then he or she might as well train and foster human capital, which is true.

DNA of the SBI Group's Corporate Culture

If a company undergoes significant changes in its management situation and such changes are sustained for some time to come, then, needless to say, the company's corporate culture will also need a significant makeover. Nonetheless, I am quite certain that the following four elements of our corporate culture must be passed down into the future as the DNA of the SBI Group (see Exhibit 4.6).

1. Continuously carry on with our entrepreneurship, or our venture capitalist spirit. We must not succumb to the "big company syndrome," wherein a company spends a significant amount of time and energy on internal management rather than external management, and must constantly take on new challenges without fear of failure.
2. Focus on speed. We must ensure that every member of the SBI Group companies always places a priority on speedy decision making and action.

3. Facilitate innovation. Without having too much attachment to past experiences of success, each top management executive must set clear innovation-focused goals and establish various institutional mechanisms to motivate all members of the SBI Group companies to continuously maximize their creative spirit.

4. Continuous self-evolution. All the SBI Group companies must at all times be keenly alert to environmental changes and flexibly adapt to them. Through self-denial and self-transformation, they must continue to work toward achieving new growth.

To ensure that these four DNA elements will be passed on into the future, the top management executive in each generation must be aware that he or she has the exceptionally important duty of establishing a group strategy for personnel, organizational matters, and other areas of the company, and for developing an appropriate corporate culture. I believe that, through such a process, a strong corporate group will be able to sustain itself.

Continuously carry on entrepreneurship (Entrepreneurship)

Focus on speed (Speed)

Facilitate innovation (Innovation)

Continuously self-evolution (Self-evolution)

EXHIBIT 4.6   DNA Elements of the SBI Group's Corporate Value to Be Passed Down into the Future

Social Contribution as a Strategic Investment

In the world of classical economics, which is premised on perfect competition prevailing among companies, profits are maximized when output is at a level where marginal revenue is equal to marginal cost, and the market mechanism, or what is known as an "invisible hand," functions to realize the effective allocation of resources. In such a world, private interests are linked to public interests, and, therefore, social equity can be realized. Under classical business management, which is based on classical economics, a company can simply ignore its employees or customers as long as it undertakes moves that are the most advantageous to the owners of the company.

Business Management in the Real World

In the real world in which we live, however, the market mechanism does not function effectively. Therefore, private interests never come to match public interests. As a result, we will need a new type of business management based on a more realistic and novel view of corporations. Under current mainstream business management, the top management executive of a company is not considered an agent for the owner of the company. Rather, he or she must coordinate the interests of interested parties who are commonly referred to as stakeholders, such as the shareholders, employees, customers, business partners, and local communities associated with that company, and must undertake efforts to activate a corporate value creation process.

Such changes in economics or business management concepts are typically brought on as well by major transformations taking place in the real world of economics. Perfect competition, which was assumed to exist in classical economics and business management in bygone days, and the market mechanism that was thought to work in the presence of perfect competition, as well as the effective allocation of resources that was supposed to be realized through the said mechanism all ceased to function properly as a result of subsequent changes in actual economies. In other words, they stopped working over time as a result of the separation of ownership from management, the emergence of large-scale organizations, and the advancement of oligopolies, among other factors.

Role of a Corporation as a Member of Society

Now then, let us give a little consideration to what a corporation is. It goes without saying that a corporation is an aggregate of individuals. An organization that represents an aggregate of individuals has far more power than individuals acting on their own. This view is exactly consistent with a proposition in complexity science: "A whole, which is composed of multiple parts, must be greater than the aggregate of its parts." In addition, a corporation is also referred to as a "juridical person." In much the same way as an individual possesses a "character," a corporation also possesses a "juridical character." This view is also consistent with another proposition that characterizes complexity studies: "A whole contains new characteristics that cannot be found in the multiple parts that comprise the whole."

Such corporate organization in the modern age functions as a core economic system in capitalistic society, and in this sense, a corporation may also be described as a part of a whole that is society. In principle, the activities undertaken by a corporation bring about various effects in society, and a corporation itself represents a social presence and one element of society. As long as a corporation continues to assume such a role, it must strive to create a harmony among the interests of the various stakeholders associated with it for both public benefit and private benefit, and must continue to exist as a going concern in solidarity with society.

Next, I briefly explain the characterization of the main stakeholders, who comprise the participants in a corporate organization, from a corporation's point of view, before making my point.

Changes in the Characterization of Stakeholders from a Corporate Perspective

For quite a long time, the Japanese view of corporations had placed a particular emphasis on customers and employees from among all types of stakeholders. However, it became obvious during the 1990s, which is often referred to as the "lost decade," that such a view was beginning to change. This period of time is defined by the burst of the massive bubble economy in Japan and the subsequent deep economic slump that was accompanied by deflationary pressures. It is no wonder, then, that the characterization of stakeholders underwent explicit changes.

Let me add a more concrete explanation of how these changes took place. The collapse of the bubble brought on the gradual disappearance of the unique nature of the traditional cross-shareholding structure, under which a comfortable majority of shares of a company was owned by financial institutions, usually the main bankers to the company, and business partners. Companies were no longer able to treat their shareholders as silent shareholders. In addition, a series of various corporate scandals that occurred around that time began to raise questions about the traditional role of corporate governance. More specifically, a number of companies came under criticism for having turned their board of directors into an exclusive buddies' club with agendas where things all too often got swept under the rug.

Under the circumstances, a new movement emerged that called for the implementation of U.S.-style corporate governance in order to restore management soundness. For example, a number of companies began to introduce a series of various new measures, such as the strengthening of a corporate auditor's role, the appointment of external directors, the introduction of an executive officer system, the installment of various new committees, and so on. In addition, many companies adopted management methods that emphasized cash flows and corporate value, with a lot of attention paid to shareholders. On the other hand, many companies, amidst the unprecedented deep economic slump, found themselves with no choice but to implement a large-scale restructuring in order to survive, and they began to replace the lifetime employment system and the customary seniority-based promotion system of Japanese companies with an early retirement system and a performance-based pay system. Because a majority of labor unions in Japan are formed within individual companies, which makes them much less powerful than their counterparts in Europe and the United States, they did not express any strong resistance to any of these changes that managements were implementing. As a result, a number of companies paid much less attention to their employees than previously.

So then, how did the characterization of customers, as one group of stakeholders, change? The answer is that an increasing number of companies began to pay more attention to their customers; the accountability bar had been raised. As I mentioned much earlier, as the expansion of the Internet community continued, a consumer sovereignty started to form, and as a result, a lot of companies simply could not survive without strict adherence to the customer-centric principle. In addition, customers were no longer looked at as just customers as in days of old, but instead they started to have a significant input into the development of new products and services.

This has now reached the point where companies are finding it very difficult, without carrying on a dialogue with their customers (such dialogue has been made a lot easier nowadays thanks to the popularity of Internet bulletin boards and weblogs, as well as company web sites that allow users to ask questions and raise issues), to develop products that can meet a wide range of customer needs.

As suggested by the term "prosumer" (a combination of "producer" and "consumer"), coined by futurist Alvin Toffler, a new trend has begun wherein producers and consumers are working together to create new products and services. It is against this background that more and more companies are placing their highest priority on their customers from among all stakeholders.

Furthermore, I understand that in Europe and the United States there are publications that rate the social nature of various companies, and some consumers are using these publications to choose socially conscious brands with respect to daily necessities and food products.

So far, I have talked in general terms of how companies have changed the way that they characterize their main stakeholders as they have come to face environmental changes. Now, let's turn to discussing how a company views its corporate social responsibility and how the SBI Group plans to fulfill its corporate social responsibility and make a contribution to society.

Social Contribution in the Context of Corporate Social Responsibility

The term "CSR (corporate social responsibility)" (see Exhibit 4.7) has frequently popped up in newspapers and magazines since 2003, which some call "CSR's debut year." A number of books have been published with the term CSR used as part of their titles. Major companies have established an internal organization that is responsible for CSR and have even begun issuing CSR reports. Nowadays, CSR is practically used as a password among management executives.

CSR has been translated as Kigyo no Shakaiteki Sekinin in Japanese, and this subject has actually been hotly debated among corporate management executives for quite some time. I remember having

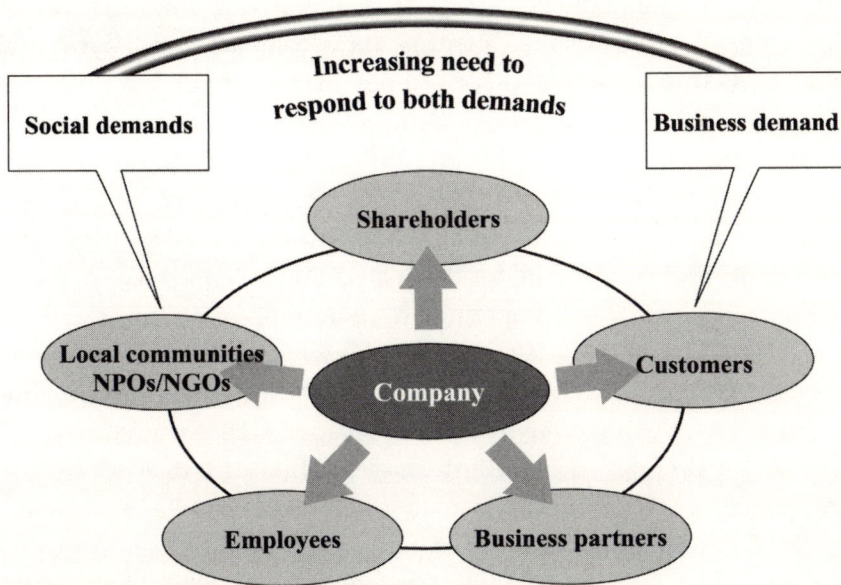

EXHIBIT 4.7 Background of the Increased Attention to Corporate Social Responsibility (CSR)

read about a company's social responsibility with deep emotion in the book *Ashita no Kigyo ni Nani ga Aruka* (*What Awaits Enterprises Tomorrow?*) by Konosuke Matsushita (PHP Institute, Inc., Tokyo, 1975). I have also read a reprinted edition of this book in *Kigyo no Shakaiteki Sekinin Towa Nanika?* (*What Is the Social Responsibility of Enterprises?*) (PHP Institute, Inc., Tokyo, 1974). I learned that Matsushita had written this book in 1974 for non-publication purposes and I was amazed at how completely original his words sound even to this day. They are so right on target even from the point of view of contemporary discussion, and I was deeply touched once again by his great wisdom.

In these writings, Matsushita says that the fundamental responsibility of a company is to make a contribution to society through the operation of its primary businesses and that other various corporate responsibilities are derived from this fundamental responsibility. The second of these derived responsibilities is to "nurture people." Matsushita argues that the nurturing of people is absolutely critical for a company in fulfilling its social responsibilities and that the basic principle of human capital development is "for a company to be accurately aware of its true mission and consistently make this mission known to all employees."

The other social responsibilities of a company suggested by Matsushita include "harmony with the local community and surrounding environments," "control and elimination of public hazards," "consideration to the reduction of under-populated and overpopulated areas," "pursuit of free and fair competition," "promotion of diplomacy by the people," and "earning adequate profits." While these responsibilities represent everything that any CSR program should strive for, allow me to supplement them with two additional responsibilities.

The first is compliance with the law and behavior that is based on a proper corporate ethic. This is an important responsibility that should be added in light of the number of corporate scandals occurring in recent years. In particular, on the front line where actual businesses are carried out, we need to implement rigorous compliance measures and establish a code of conduct in order to prevent employees from acting in an unethical manner or against social conventions, even with respect to matters that are not legally prohibited.

The second is the fulfillment of social responsibility through philanthropy, and *mécénat*, a French word for corporate support of the arts, both of which became quite common in the 1990s. Philanthropy means to give back to society the profits that are earned by a company through various donations and other charitable activities, participation in the community, and volunteer activities in local communities, among other forms. *Mécénat*, on the other hand, refers to social contribution activities that place a focus on making contributions to the arts and culture. All of these activities have been actively undertaken primarily by companies in the United States and Europe. In Japan, the long-standing mainstream view has always been to fulfill corporate social responsibilities through business activities, as seconded by Matsushita's view referred to earlier.

I believe, however, that we should also actively engage in philanthropic and *mécénat*-like activities. To this end, in January 2002 the SBI Group established a basic policy for undertaking direct social contribution activities and so far has provided donations, mainly to childcare centers and infant homes (see Exhibit 4.8).

I am fairly certain that the CSR activities that are undertaken by Japanese corporations today have changed quite significantly since the days Matsushita was actively involved in business management. To put it differently, in the old days there was a predominant view that a company should conduct its CSR activities to fulfill its social responsibilities, whereas today CSR activities are viewed in a more positive light as a strategic investment to achieve an increase in corporate value on a sustained basis.

Moreover, in recent years there has even been the view that a company should encourage its customers to transform themselves, which in turn can create new social values and, ultimately, social reform.

Such conceptual changes are attributed to changes in the values that are held by the various stakeholders associated with each company. This means that customers and shareholders, as well as the employees and business partners of a company, not to mention local

October 2005   **The SBI Children's Hope**
                      Foundation was established.

March 2005   **Donations made to entities that support**
                      the intermediate corporation:
                      SBI received shares in a newly publicly held company from its
                      founder, as well as new stock option rights in an unlisted company.

January 2005   **Start of full-fledged activities by the SBI Child Welfare**
                      Limited Liability Intermediate Corporation:
                      SBI toured and learned about facilities nationwide, and visited and interviewed
                      local governments across Japan.

December 2004   **Establishment of the SBI Child Welfare Limited Liability**
                      Intermediate Corporation:
                      In addition to donations from each group company, SBI became the first enterprise
                      in Japan to donate stock options and to actively use the securities market for CSR.

July 2004   **Start of full-fledged donation activities:**
                      After receiving the support of nine special government ordinance-designated cities and 39
                      prefectures, SBI donated 167.1 million yen (173 facilities) to childcare centers and infant
                      homes that are under the jurisdiction of local governments.

January 2002   **Establishment of a basic policy by Softbank Finance's board of**
                      directors:
                      Each group company that earns over three hundred million yen in net income donates 1% of
                      its profits to the facilities for children.

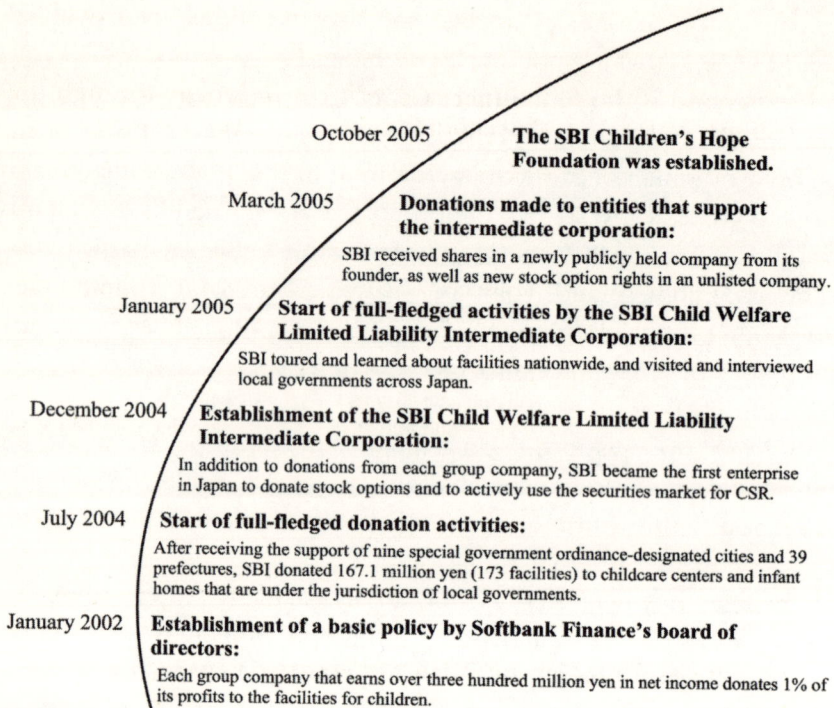

EXHIBIT 4.8   Direct Social Contribution Activities of the SBI Group

communities, have come to attach an importance to the social nature
of that company. At the SBI Group, rather than placing an emphasis on
the social significance of CSR activities, we undertake efforts to increase the understanding of CSR activities by internally expressing their
strategic significance from the perspective of our values.

Continuous Enhancement of Corporate Value Through CSR Activities

As stated earlier, the SBI Group defines its corporate value as the aggregate of customer value, shareholder value, and human capital
value. It is our view that through CSR activities we will increase each
of these forms of value to ultimately enhance our corporate value (see
Exhibit 4.9).

1 **Increase in customer value**	2 **Increase in shareholder value**	3 **Increase in human capital value**
Positive impact can be created for increasingly socially conscious customers through an improved reputation relating to social contribution.	Increased long-term business opportunities through socially responsible investment (SRI), or aggressive social contribution activities, and synergies can be created with customer value and human capital value.	Loyalty can be raised among existing officers and employees, and an improved ability to externally recruit superior human capital.

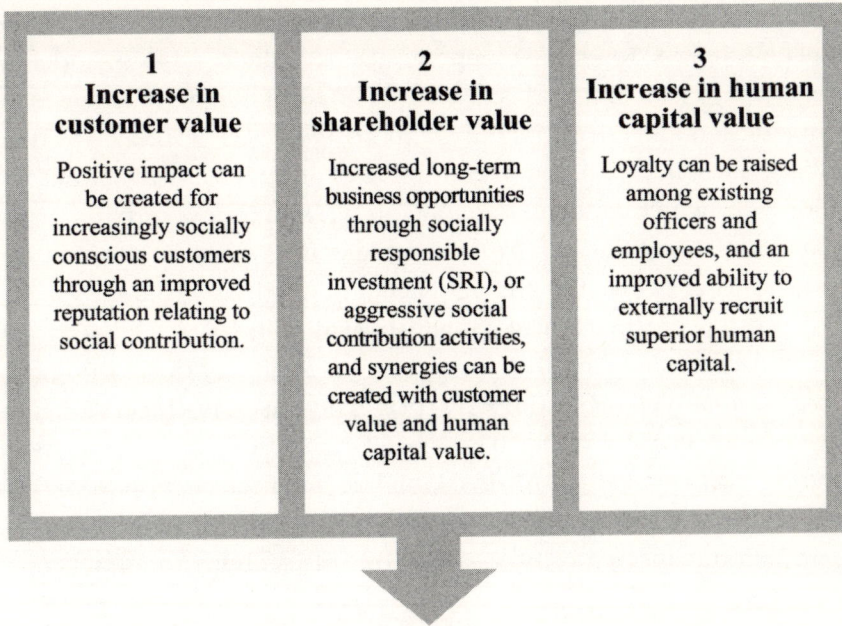

Social contribution activities = Strategic investment

EXHIBIT 4.9   Significance of Social Contribution Efforts

Through an improvement in its reputation as a company that makes a social contribution, a company is able to increase its customer value by having a positive impact on the consumption and investing activities of increasingly socially conscious customers. The SBI Group engages in activities to promote child welfare with a groupwide determination. These activities may also be looked at as a tool for breaking into the next generation of customers.

Regarding shareholder value, a company that rigorously emphasizes compliance is relatively less likely to face a risk that its stock price will drop in the event of a scandal in comparison to a company that does not place as much importance on compliance.

In addition, socially responsible investment (SRI), which has been around for some time in the United States and Europe, is gradually drawing attention in Japan, and a series of SRI funds, which invest in companies that are known for their superior CSR activities, have been launched. In fact, for some companies to have their stocks included in the portfolio of an SRI fund is one of the goals of their CSR activities, or it provides an incentive for taking a more aggressive approach to their CSR activities. In Japan, the overall value of SRI funds is only about 267 billion yen, which fades in comparison with their counterparts in the United States and Europe. In the United States, the total value of SRI funds has already reached the equivalent of nearly 260 trillion yen.

From the perspective of human capital value, CSR activities can also be useful for raising the motivation and loyalty of the existing officers and employees of a company. This is because the officers and employees of a company that has a good reputation for making social contributions are likely to receive a high level of satisfaction from their jobs. In addition, a company that is highly involved in making a social contribution is more advantaged in terms of its ability to attract supe-

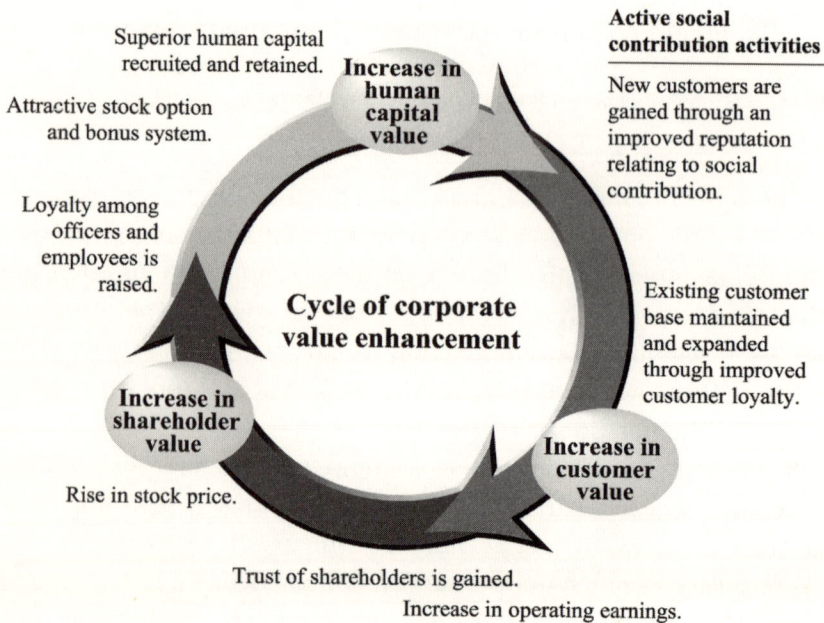

EXHIBIT 4.10   Social Contribution Facilitates a Virtuous Cycle of Corporate Value Enhancement

rior human capital. New graduates who are entering the work force nowadays more frequently than ever give consideration to whether their prospective employers are socially conscious.

In this way, it may be said that CSR activities can have a positive impact on each of the aforementioned three forms of value. If such is the case, then these three forms of value can facilitate the enhancement of a company's corporate value through mutual linkage with each other (see Exhibit 4.10).

As Matsushita has suggested, social contribution through the operation of the primary businesses of a company forms the foundation for the CSR activities of that company. We should once again recognize that it is important above all to undertake every effort to ensure that these three forms of value will continuously increase through our primary businesses. We must remember that such a goal is possible only if we work in concert to perform day-to-day with integrity and under a sound management philosophy.

AUTHOR PROFILE

1951: Born in Hyogo Prefecture, Japan.

1974: Graduated from Keio University, Japan, and joined Nomura Securities Co., Ltd.

1978: Graduated from Cambridge University, England.

1989: Appointed Managing Director of Wasserstein Perella & Co. International, Limited (London)

1991: Appointed Director of Nomura Wasserstein Perella Co., Ltd.

1992: Appointed Corporate Finance & Services Dept. III General Manager, Nomura Securities Co., Ltd.

1995: Appointed Executive Vice President and Chief Financial Officer of SOFTBANK CORP.

Present: Appointed Representative Director and CEO of SBI Holdings, Inc.

SBI Holdings, Inc. is an integrated financial group that is comprised of various subsidiaries operating innovative financial businesses, such as SBI Investment Co., Ltd., which is a venture capital firm, SBI E*TRADE SECURITIES Co., Ltd., which is an online securities firm, and SBI Mortgage Co., Ltd., which offers housing loans with a securitized 35-year fixed interest rate, among others.

Other books by the author are: *Chugoku Koten kara Moratta "Fushigi na Chikara"* (*"Mysterious Powers" Gained from Chinese Classics*), Mikasa Shobo Co., Ltd., Tokyo, 2005; *"Kachi Sozo" no Keiei*

(*"Value-Creation" Management*), Toyo Keizai Inc., Tokyo, 1997; *E-fainansu no Chosen* (*Challenges of E-Finance*), Toyo Keizai Inc., Tokyo, 1999; *E-fainansu no Chosen II* (*Challenges of E-Finance II*), Toyo Keizai Inc., Tokyo, 2000; *Fuhen no Keiei, Seicho no Keiei* (*Universal Management, Growth Management*), PHP Institute, Inc., Tokyo, 2000; and *Jinbutsu o Tsukuru* (*Developing Character*), PHP Institute, Inc., Tokyo, 2003.

INDEX

157